THE SPACE OF THE WAIST ®

BOOK 1 - THE GUIDE BOOK

YOUR FASHION GUIDE BASED ON BODY SHAPE AND THE SPACE OF THE WAIST®

This Guide Book along with all 18 books within the complete series for your Body Shape and THE SPACE OF THE WAIST® is available for download/purchase on: www.amazon.com/author/melodyedmondson

Follow THE SPACE OF THE WAIST® on:
Facebook - www.facebook.com/thespaceofthewaist
Pinterest - www.pinterest.com/christamelody/the-space-of-the-waist
Website/Blog - www.thespaceofthewaist.com

THE SPACE OF THE WAIST®

BOOK 1 - THE GUIDE BOOK

YOUR FASHION GUIDE
BASED ON BODY SHAPE &
THE SPACE OF THE WAIST®

C. Melody Edmondson, Msc.D.
MJP ©2015

Published by MJP Publishing Inc., 2015
Attn. Melody Edmondson 12112 N. Rancho Vistoso Blvd. Tucson, AZ.
85755 | email: thespaceofthewaist@gmail.com

Library of Congress Cataloging-in-Publication Data
10 9 8 7 6 5 4 3 edition
Copyright © 2015. All rights reserved.
Edmondson, Melody

Book 1 - The Guide Book: Your Fashion Guide Based on your
Body Shape and THE SPACE OF THE WAIST®
Lexicon and Indices for complete book series included in Book 1 -
The Guide Book: Your Fashion Guide Based on Body Shape and
THE SPACE OF THE WAIST®

CREDITS
Book Copy Editing by Simone Gers and Sandy Marie.
Cover Design, Interior Formatting/Layout, and Figure Illustrations by
David A. Russell via Studio DRive C_ | www.studiodrivec.com

DEDICATION TO MY MOTHER

This Guide Book and its series of eighteen books are dedicated to my beautiful, creative Mother, Marilyn Grace McClure Place.

With her belief and consistent encouragement throughout my lifetime, I stretched my boundaries and accomplished what I have.

Without her steadfast ethical and spiritual inner grace, I never would have found my inner peace. Without her generosity, highly creative spirit, know-how, and her unfailing love, I am not sure I could have survived the outside world, as a sensitive.

Also, I never would have known about the fairies who lived in the clover nor the angels who slept in my top bunk. I may not ever have had such deep appreciation for all of God's many ways of helping. Mother had a great imagination, and it was a gift to her children. We learned to stretch our minds and see *into* people and situations.

It is my deepest belief that if we have aware and conscious parents, who are correlated deeply with the abilities and dispositions of their children, they can guide their children to their greatest heights both spiritually as well as professionally.

I did, however, spend much time as a very young child, with Mother. She was a stay at home mother. It was 1951 when I came into the world, December 25th on Christmas Day. "Creative Motherhood" was my mother's career. She excelled greatly as she was an astute artist, decorator, and Designer of high fashion apparel, AND she was a "Fashion Diva" (like her talented mother before her, Vivian Belle Cox McClure). This fashion forward sense developed in me through Mother served me well in my fashion careers that followed.

I was taught I was capable of figuring the most important things out for myself, with God within helping me. It was up to me to follow my heart and passions and to think in the moment. New trails may often need to be blazed, perhaps even mid-stream as life is happening, and they may interrupt one's plans. The joy and the key is to be inside any given moment. Being inside any artistic, creative task or situation means becoming fully involved. I was being taught to think and act in the NOW.

I was shown how to be ingenious, how to scramble, how to look ahead with foresight, and how to achieve my goals and dreams in life. I was taught to sell and how to sell myself. I was taught how to know my own strengths and weakness and to continually improve upon myself. I was shown how to be thoughtful, generous, inclusive, and gracious, and how to be a survivor.

Mother encouraged and believed in each of us wholeheartedly. I was shown I had value and to TRUST my inner voice, my inner guidance. Mother called this conscience. Mother believed God was everywhere. We were to rely on *this* guidance forever.

Through Mother's loving presence, special regard, her inherent belief in God, her ability to create beauty wherever she goes, her many talents, her personal inner and outer beauty, and her sincere devotion to me, I acknowledge the "Blessed Gift" of my unique mother, and I dedicate this book, and the book series, to my mother, Marilyn Grace McClure Place.

SECTIONS LIST

Dedication to my Mother

Acknowledgements

Introduction to THE SPACE OF THE WAIST®

Lexicon for the Fashion and Women's Apparel Industry

A Woman's Figure / Body Shape:
- o   The Body Shapes, Unchangeables, Primary Modifiers
- o   IT IS NOT about Weight, IT IS about Fit and Waistplacement
- o   Silhouette Tips for Short-waisted and Long-waisted Women

Overview of Individual Body Shapes

How to measure in order to determine the Body Shape

How to measure for THE SPACE OF THE WAIST® and Waistplacement

What's TORSO got to do with Waistplacement?

What's STRIDE got to do with Fit?

What are My *ASSETS*?

Formulas for Eye-breaks / Creating with Layers of Clothing

Waistplacement Formulas applied to the Body Shapes
- o   The Fashion Industries Answer...

Conclusion - Locating your book for *your* Body Shape and Waistplacement

Indices, needed for each book within the series:
- I.   Color Groups
- II. Fabric Choices
- III. Prints & Patterns
- IV. Embellishments
- V.   Silhouettes and details used throughout complete book series

Author Bio& Complete Book List

ILLUSTRATIONS LIST

A complete list of all illustrations organized by Sections List.
All figures illustrated by David A. Russell via Studio Drive C_.

Female Body Shape:
- o   Figure 1

Body Shapes by Waistplacement:
- o   Figures 2-19

How to Measure the...
- o   Body Shape by Sections: Figure 20
- o   Shoulders: Figure 21
- o   Bust: Figure 22
- o   Waist: Figure 23
- o   Hips: Figure 24

SPACE OF THE WAIST®:
- o   Measuring Area: Figure 20
- o   BSL Waistplacement: Figures 21, 22, and 23

Measuring the TORSO:
- o   Figures 24, 25, 26, and 27

Measuring STRIDE:
- o   Measurement area: Figure 33 a/b
- o   Stride area on BSL: Figures 34, 35, and 36

Line Break Examples for Layers 4, 3, 2, and 1:
- o   Figures 37, 38, 39, and 40

ACKNOWLEDGEMENTS

I wish to express my deep gratitude to the special people who made this book possible. Without their expertise and support, I would not have been able to properly execute *The Guide Book* and the 18 books within *The Book Series*.

Former CEO Bernard Zindler was my very first boss. I had the privilege of becoming a Buyer for Better Juniors and Contemporary Sportswear for the specialty store Swanson's on the Plaza in Kansas City Missouri. "Bernie" guided me and taught me more than I could begin to elaborate but I will reveal he was the best at explaining to me all about the torso and it's three waist positions. Thanks for everything "Bernie." It would be remiss to mention Swanson's without also sending my praises to two of my strongest sales-team members Edith Freidman and Regina Pactor.

Thank you to the *sacred* Simone Gers for editing *The Guide Book* and some of the books within *The Book Series*. Simone also made contributions to all of the books within *The Book Series*. Simone's suggestions led to the development of a separate book, *The Guide Book,* and each of the Body Shapes by Waistplacement books, standing alone as individual books, versus an all-in-one book. Simone has taught me much and not just about book writing.

Thank you to my dear friend, Sandy Marie, for the final editing of *The Book Series*, to include *The Guide Book*. Also, special thanks to Sandy, for being such a beautiful fashion ICON, artist and an inspiration to all fashionistas.

Most importantly, I have been blessed to have had the technologically savvy, David A. Russell owner and Creative Director of Studio DRive C_, as my Cover Designer, Illustrator and Production Manager for *The Guide Book* and *The Book Series* (18) expressing THE SPACE OF THE WAIST®. David is talented beyond what space could allow.

"There is usually a way to adapt a fashion trend for your Body Shape and Waistplacement. But…when it comes to daily dressing, IT IS your WAISTPLACEMENT not seasonal trends and not your weight that is the defining factor for your clothing selections."

- C. Melody Edmondson

THE SPACE OF THE WAIST®

The Guide Book is the first book in the series and should be read first, in order for you to discover or verify your Body Shape and your Waistplacement.

"**THE SPACE OF THE WAIST**®" will help you find your unique Body Shape and your personal **WAISTPLACEMENT** which determines how *much* space is available in your waist area. This knowledge provides valuable insight into your clothing, fashion, Silhouette and accessory choices. *Waistplacement* is essential to style/garment/apparel or what I refer to as **SILHOUETTE** selection as the waist modifies the Body Shape very dramatically. Once you discover if you are Balanced, Short or Long-waisted, your selections become easy.

Body Shape correlated to Waistplacement is uncovered territory at the Wholesale, Manufacturing and Retail Store levels of the Women's Apparel Industry. It is time for an **INDUSTRY CHANGE.** Once women demand Long-waisted and Short-waisted clothing/apparel in their Silhouette choices, the **Retailers** will encourage and inform the Designers and Manufacturers in the Apparel Industry and The Fashion World will transform. Consumer demand will get the ball rolling in the 21st Century. My goal for Retail Store availability of Short and Long Waist Silhouettes by classifications is 2018 or soon thereafter.

Now that you have read Book One: *The Guide Book* and have downloaded/ purchased the proper book for your individual Body Shape with its associating Waistplacement, you can begin to learn how to best flatter your Body Shape and Waistplacement. Your best Silhouettes, tips for layering, and the building of your Basic Black Wardrobe in Trans-Seasonal Fabrics are provided. Also included, is a guide to *your* Shopping Cycles & Shopping List/Recap.

A LEXICON FOR THE FASHION AND WOMEN'S APPAREL INDUSTRY

Vocabulary used in the Fashion Industry, not commonly found in dictionaries.

For the purpose of this book as a knowledge-gathering tool, a lexicon has been created. The lexicon is comprised of both words commonly used by the Fashion and Women's Apparel Industries, and additional much-needed words I coined. This lexicon is used throughout this Guide Book and the 18 books of *The Book Series that* are available simultaneously. I also use a non-grammatically correct DRAMA of Capitalized Letters and WORDS when I feel it is important to excite extreme emphasis. I am hoping to use these words and phrases to draw the reader into her most flattering and essential holism, while using the visible female's Body Shape and Waistplacement *image* as her medium of expression.

WORDS WILL SOMETIMES BE FOUND CAPITALIZED IN FULL *or in Part, AS THEY ARE DEEMED VIABLE* to their level of SIGNIFICANCE, AS "KEY WORDS", TO THE STATEMENTS EXPRESSED.

LEXICON

WAISTPLACEMENT TERMS FOR USE IN ALL CLOTHING AND BODY SHAPES OF FEMALE BODIES:

Waistplacement (versus waist placement or waist-placement)
Balanced-waist(ed) or Balanced Waistplacement = B
Short-waist(ed) or Short Waistplacement = S
Long-waist(ed) or Long Waistplacement = L
Waisted(s) or waistedness(es) refers to the Waistplacement

WAISTLINE FOR TOPS/DRESSES/TROUSERS/SKIRTS AND SOME COATS:

Drop-waist(s) / Dropped-waisted(s): A waist that is dropped to a lower level to camouflage where the Natural-waist occurs on the body.
Empired: right under the bustline.
Highwaist(s) / Highwaisted(s): A Waistline that is high and defined.
Raised-Waistline: A Waistline that is above the Normal-waistline.
Waistless: no defined waist.

DETAILS FOR TOPS/DRESSES/JACKETS AND SOME COATS:

Besom: an elongated buttonhole looking pocket.
Empired: empire waisted. Fit is under the bust versus at the waist.
Shoulder-Empire: fitted/shirred/placed at the shoulder, then flowing.
Neck-Empire: fitted/shirred/placed at the neckline, then flowing.
Eyebreak(s): used in formulas such as clothing hemlines, creating the break; an accessory, color, collar, etc., causing the eye to break on the body, versus a linear flow.
Faggotted: cut work
Flippy: flipped up
Floaty: flowing and easy
Flowy: swaying and easy
Lettuced: curved and rippled
Lettucing: curving and rippling
Tuliped: tulip shaped at the bottom hem
Poof (Poofy, poofing, poofiness, poofed): ballooning, bellowing or fuller
Shirtings: shirts in menswear fabrics
Shoulderlines: the line of the shoulder

Skirtsuit or pantsuit: a skirt with a matching/coordinated jacket, or a pant with a matching/coordinated jacket.

Suede(s): soft-finished leather

Stitched-down-pleated (stitched-down-pleats, stitched-down and then pleated): Stiched down to create a flat front, and then pleated.

TOPS/DRESS/COATS:

Empired: Silhouettes using the fit under the bust versus the waist.

Shirtings: Menswear, woven shirts in solids or patterns/prints/stripes.

Tee-shirt/T-shirt: Refers to a cotton-knit top, usually with stretch; in 1950's termed a tee-top but modernly referred to as a tee-shirt or T-shirt.

Turtlenecked: Referring to turtle neck tops.

Turnback: Cuffs that turnback.

Vee-neck(s), Vee-neckline(s), Veed-neckline(s) or neck(s), Vee(s), V-neck(s): A top with a veed neckline.

SWIMWEAR:

Mio(s): Maillot-type swimsuit Silhouette with a scooped neck, plain simple bodice and curved higher leg cuts.

Monokini(s): A cut-out one-piece swimsuit Silhouette in which the cut outs often resemble an hourglass.

Tankini(s): A 2-piece swimsuit Silhouette that appears to be a 1-piece suit. The top fits much like a camisole and the bottom like a bikini or full swimsuit bottom.

FABRICS AND MATERIALS:

Charmeuse(s): a satin-finished silk fabric with shine. This fabric may be used on the reverse side, as well, for a comfortable, luxurious feeling.

Metallics: Accessories, fabric, color, notions, embellishments or trims when used in the plural for the word metallic

Opaques: hosiery in opaque color, used as a plural.

Tweed(ed): Tweeds, or small inter-looping threads, usually fabrics for jackets/coats/trousers and skirts.

Viscose(es) and Acetate(s): Blended man-made fabrics.

COLORS:

Any color may have many pigmentations of its hue; therefore, plural forms in all colors are used.

Aquas: plural of aqua as a color

Fuschia(s): A bright pink color often spelled this way. Designers use the spelling **fuschia** versus the fuchsia spelling because, as one female Designer told me, of its "prettier" appeal.

Golds: gold, plural

Metallics: The metal colors in fabrics, singular or plural.

Euro-dusted Darks: Dark deep colors merged into other colors, or dusted colorations and pigments.

Neon(s): A bright acid color of which there are many.

Platinums: platinum, plural

Seafoam(s): A color as one-word that may be plural of which there are a number of pigmentations and variations.

Taupes: plural of the color taupe, several in this pigmentation.

PATTERNS/PRINTS:

Florals: Patterns with flowers are referred to as florals in the Apparel or Fashion Industry.

Houndstooth(s): An angled rectangle all-over pattern on a ground color.

Prints and Patterns: Including graphics, geometrics, florals, and other creations in forms of prints, patterns and stripes.

STRIDES OF TROUSERS OR JEANS:

Stride(s) and Strided(s): the crotch of a trouser or jean, jegging or legging. It is common in the Fashion or Retail Industry to refer to a woman as short or long strided.

Long Stride(s) or Long Strided

Short Stride(s) or Short Strided

WORDS USED IN DESCRIPTIVE FORMS:

Monochromatic(s): color tones/pigments of the same hue, often worn in varying pigments together in one-look.

Pluraled: plural in the past tense

Silhouette(s): A specific garment in a specific style or shape.

Unbulky: Anything, particularly an item of clothing, that does not make the body appear thicker.

Mini: Shorter than average skirt, dress, or coat.

Maxi: Longer to the ankle in length dress, skirt, coat, vest, jacket or top.

Leaner: Silhouettes are often shaped. The idea is a longer in length Silhouette that is narrow.

Priceline: Prices have ranges and the range is a priceline.

Straightline(s) and Straighterlines(ed): Lines are straight moving.

Long lines and Longlined: Lines moving in a vertical direction.

Rouching(s): Gathering that is engineered by design.

"Speedy Type": references the Louis Vuitton top handled SPEEDY bag.

Wearings: More than one wearing.

Detailings: Detailing pluraled.

Seasonless: Fabrics and Silhouettes that may be worn in any season.

Bootcut: The slightly shorter and flared trouser or jean leg cut.

FEATURES, PEOPLE, GROUPS OR INDIVIDUALS:

Unchangeables: Features you cannot change, such as Waistplacement, height, frame, arm/leg length, foot/hand size, and neck length.

Borderliners: women who are nearly one Body Shape or another, or nearly one Waistplacement or another. An example of a Borderliner Triangle Shape is a woman who has slightly narrower shoulders than hips, but who may insert shoulder pads to appear as an Hourglass Body Shape. For instance, a woman may only be 1/2 or 1-inch off from having Balanced Waistplacement. If you are less than an inch off from having a Balanced-waist, you may "fudge" the belt to appear Balanced-waisted.

ABOUT THE FEMALE BODY:

Bustline(s): The breasts/breast area of a garment or of the body itself.

Hipline(s): The hip area of a garment or the body itself.

Skirtline(s): Lines of a skirt bodice or hemline.

Shoulderline(s): Lines at the shoulder of a Silhouette.

Waistline(s): Waist of a garment or the body itself.

THE BODY SHAPES:
Circle: A rounder Body Shape.

Hourglass(es) or Double Triangle(ed): An Inverted Triangle situated at the top half of the body and a Triangle at the bottom half. The shoulders and hips are about the same measurement, and the waist is 10-inches smaller than the hips/shoulders.

Inverted Triangle(ed): A shape in which the shoulders are significantly wider than the hips. This shape resembles an upside-down Triangle.

Rectangle(ed): A linear Body Shape with shoulders, waist and hips all about the same measurement.

Square: A Body Shape for which the shoulders and hips are wider (ample not narrow) or both are about the same width. Usually, the waist is wider and the legs are shorter.

Triangle(ed): A Triangle Body Shape featuring narrower shoulders than hips. Much like an Hourglass except the shoulders are considerably narrower than the hips.

IMPORTANT WORDS USED TO DESCRIBE THE FOLLOWING WORK:
Formulas: Formulas for 4, 3, 2 or 1 line(s) or eyebreak(s). Eyebreaks are created through lines of detail on the clothing or from layered hemlines of the garments worn. For instance, a collar featured under another top creates one layer over another layer with differing hemlines thus creates two separate eyebreaks or lines. Formulas in eyebreaks may be used in order to flatter the Body Shape and Waistplacement.

Gestalt: means an "all at once KNOWING." The knowing is either, yes, this is good, or no, this is not good. The no and the yes are referenced in relation to looks or Silhouettes on a Body Shape and an individual woman's Waistplacement.

Skew(s)/Askew(ed): To move the eye elsewhere. To throw-off the eye by readjusting the bodyline through Silhouettes and/or their various hemlines.

A WOMAN'S FIGURE/BODY SHAPE

A woman's Body Shape is commonly termed "her figure." The Body Shape includes all of the following: frame and bone size (some women are small, some medium, and some large boned), soft tissue, frame, water mass (or dehydration), lean body mass and muscle mass (BMI). All of *these together create the Body Shape.*

The CHANGEABLES, weight and weight distribution, are variable and can distort your natural Body Shape.

There are **UNCHANGEABLES as PRIMARY MODIFIERS of the Body Shape; they are height and Waistplacement.**

There are **UNCHANGEABLES** as **Secondary Modifiers** of the Body Shape. **SECONDARY MODIFIERS** are neck length, leg length, arm length, feet size, hand size, leg shape, ankle size, and bone size. These do not modify the Body Shape with the impact of height and Waistplacement.

THE BODY SHAPES UNCHANGEABLES PRIMARY MODIFIERS:
UNCHANGABLES are genetic. Various attributes cannot be altered. The **2 Key PRIMARY MODIFIERS are height and Waistplacement**. Learning to love, respect and honor these attributes is important as your lineage, heredity and the beautiful physical-plane carrier of your soul, your intelligence and your personality. They are the **GIFTS** you embody!

For the purpose of this book, height will not be overly reviewed as I feel you have a pretty good grasp of height adaptations relating to Body Shape and Proportion. It is **Waistplacement** *combined* with your Body Shape, that I feel you and the clothing industry need knowledge expansion in order to better understand and consciously address the most accurate way to clothe women in the 21st Century.

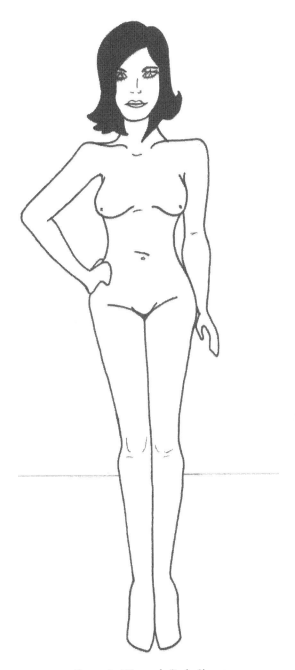

Figure 1 - Woman's Body Shape

IT IS NOT ABOUT WEIGHT -- IT IS ABOUT FIT AND WAISTPLACEMENT

Weight factors of heavier or thinner do not give the full story about Body Shape, because they leave out the Primary Modifier of the Body Shape, which is Waistplacement. All the apple-pear dialogue about Body Shape will not solve the challenges women face in finding apparel that fits and flatters, without the consideration of the **3-Waistplacements.** Much focus has been placed on weight loss, pushing anorexia and bulimia to new heights, without addressing the real issue, which is that women want to look and feel good in their clothes and bodies. With the focus on weight loss, there is a deep lack of knowledge among Designers, Vendors, Apparel Manufacturers, and, especially, Women, as it relates to Body Shape and **Unchangeable Waistplacement.** This is a Waistplacement women will live with and *clothe* for the rest of their lives. Waistplacement is very important information to integrate into the sizing of women's apparel, Silhouette by Silhouette.

Through *The Guide Book* and the 18 books in *The Book Series*, my intention is to help women value their Body Shapes and focus on what is essential: to understand how WAISTPLACEMENT is KEY to apparel fitting and flattering in a pleasing manner, and to no longer focus on forcing ourselves to achieve a Body Shape, proportion or size we were not designed to have.

Many women are simply not aware of their waist positions on their torsos. They do not understand that they are Balanced, Short or Long Waisted. The clothes on the market today are designed and manufactured for Balance-waisted women. Balance-waisted women may need support with their Body Shape, but their Waistplacement is already engineered into clothes today.

Short-waisted women are sometimes confused BECAUSE THEY OFTEN ARE TALLER AND SLIMMER WITH VERY LONG LEGS. Short-waisted women often feel, instead, that the dresses and sportswear classics do not fit them, so they must be fat. But this is not the case at all, and further dieting is not the answer for anyone who is not overweight for her BMI. Sometimes when the woman knows she is down to the bone, she is simply stumped and continues to feel bad. The answer is a simple one: she is **Short-waisted, that is the NECESSARY UNCHANGEABLE**

WAISTPLACEMENT KNOWLEDGE. Waistplacement is the reason why fitted dresses, belted dresses, fitted and flared dresses and coats, belted coats, wrap coats, belted tops, peplums and nearly all the classics, like a fitted classic blazer, or a shirtwaist dress, fit so horrifically.

Knowing *your* Waistplacement helps you answer questions like: *"why do belts at the waist look horrible on me," "Why can't I wear, a fitted at the waist dress or a cardigan sweater set?" "I cannot wear most classic Silhouettes at all because they do not fit nor look right on me. Why? I want to wear them. I have dieted but I still cannot wear a shirtwaist dress, and most jackets hit me at the wrong place on my body. A fitted peplum jacket looks funny, and all skirts/trousers/jeans with a blouse tucked in look weird. Why!"* These are the dilemmas of a Short-waisted woman. IT IS NOT A WEIGHT PROBLEM. It is, instead, a factor of Waistplacement.

Waistplacement knowledge gained and utilized for Silhouette selections will benefit all women for the rest of their lives. All women have challenges in terms of Body Shape. However, Short and Long-waisted women also have challenges related to Waistplacement because clothes are not designed with their Waistplacement in mind. Because of the challenges that Short and Long-waisted women face in view of Waistplacement, information and knowledge about Silhouette selection is essential.

SILHOUETTE SELECTION TIPS FOR <u>SHORT-WAISTED</u> WOMEN:

Short-waisted women, regardless of weight or height have an UNCHANGEABLE WAIST PLACEMENT, and this means some Silhouettes will never work on their bodies, but others will. Learning the Silhouettes and styles that work on your Short-waisted Body Shape is imperative.

Short-waisted women do not look good in the same Silhouettes as those who are Long-waisted. Short-waisted women have major challenges with anything fitted or any Silhouette ending at their waists. For daily wearing, and that means her coats, dresses, jackets, tops, skirts, trousers/jeans, and any and all classifications of merchandise that is fitted or belted at the waistline, will be the wrong Silhouettes for ALL Short-waisted women. The reason is because the waistlines of these Silhouettes in dresses, coats, jackets, tops etc. fit nearly at the Short-waisted woman's hip versus her waistline.

These belted and fitted at the waistline Silhouettes will make Short-waisted women appear shorter and wider on the top half of the body. If you wear them, you will appear very boxy and square in any of these Silhouettes, even if they are altered to fit your shape perfectly. It is not just a fit issue. The fitted at the waist Silhouettes are the wrong Silhouettes to purchase and, certainly, the wrong Silhouettes to wear. If you are Short-waisted, you will simply have to become aware that many Silhouettes will never look correct on your Waistplacement, and this means for the rest of your life. SILHOUETTE SELECTION KNOW-HOW is paramount!

Jackets for Short-waisted Women:
The top half of the Short-waisted women is usually a boxy form because of the lack of THE SPACE OF THE WAIST®. The bottom half of the Short-waisted body is usually leaner with longer legs. The marrying of the two is accomplished through an essential longer, leaner Dark Pigment jacket. A jacket of straight lines provides the best result. Jackets or gutsier-sweaters/tops are predominant pieces for the Short-waisted woman's bodyline, because they help create a visually balanced proportion.

While Jackets need to be longer and leaner in Silhouette, knits and lighter flowing fabrics and/or draping or softer fabrics are the best (the less detailing the better). Forget about any front pockets as they will hit at the hips and exaggerate the widest part of the body. Strong shoulders are wise, as shoulders and fabric set the tone of the jacket. Let the length and straight-longer line make the statement and lead the viewer to those long legs! Even with average or shorter legs, long and lean is still the wisest Silhouette to select in a jacket.

Hopefully, you found your longer and leaner jacket Silhouette in black and a knitted, gutsy fabric. If a perfect one is not found when you need it, change the look of the jacket by wearing a long to mid-thigh length, detailed, pleated or wired, ruffled or interesting scarf around the neck, hanging down the middle of the lapels. These 3.5 to 5-inch scarf streamers hanging straight will skew the eye linearly and away from the too-short, too -wide jacket.

Longer, leaner jackets teamed with narrower trousers or skirts work very well on the Short-waisted. If you are taller and leaner, you may wear wider-legged trousers and fuller skirts. Always remember to select flat-front trousers and skirts, so your tops can smoothly sit on the outside of the waistband. Wear longer, leaner tops to the lower hip-length on the outside of trousers, jeans and skirts in order to askew the eye from the too-short waist and to move the eye to a lower position visually elongating the body. This also balances the bodyline. A black fitted tank top becomes an everyday bottom-layering piece for the Short-waisted woman, because it helps askew the waistline.

Good ideas are the long over the long Silhouettes for Short-waists. A long top like a jacket or sweater over longer-leaner skirts, trousers or jeans elongates the bodyline.

Some women, if they have a fuller stomach, may layer a wider belt to the mid-belly position over a blouse in a contrasting color from the jacket. With this example, wear black, straight-legged trousers with a white mid-thigh length shirt, belted at mid-belly, and teamed with a jacket of tapestry pattern in a bright colorful print. The collarless jacket is worn open along with the open collar of the white shirt.

Jacket choices may be in brighter colors, but the wisest investment for day-to-day wear and wardrobe accumulation are darks as the fabric in Dark Pigments coordinate with dark skirts, trousers, jeans, maxis, longer and leaner dresses, and straightlined shorter dresses. This Dark-Pigment wardrobe will proportion your Body Shape/Waistplacement the best. Then, gradually, add novelties to your jacket Silhouette wardrobe.

A few choice novelties flatter the Short-waisted Bodyline: longer and leaner sweater coats, longer and leaner vests, and long, straightlined, button-front cardigans and dresses worn as jackets. The triangle / trapeze shaped jacket is a fun novelty if you can locate one in a day weight, so it can be worn for the entire day to complete your look. Often, trapeze Silhouettes are only found in outerwear weights and need to be removed once at the office, movie or dinner. Looks need to be created with the jacket left on as it is *the* essential elongation piece for the top half of the body proportion. Looks need to carry you to work, to the movies or to dinner without taking off your jacket or third layer, such as a longer ankle vest in black.

Short-waisted women must wear tops on the outside to the longer hip or thigh in length. These longer and leaner (not wide) tops will be worn over the waistbands of all of your jeans, trousers, and mini, midi, maxi or ankle skirts. If you desire, you may belt them at the hip NOT the waist. It is very important that there is absolutely no bulk at the waist of any bottom that you purchase, as the tops must hang smoothly over the waistbands and fronts of all bottoms worn. The skirts would need to be stitched-down flat, and then pleated. Skirts may not be gathered or fuller under the waistband as this creates a non-flat surface for the lower-hip length top that needs to be layered over that waist.

Hip belts elongate the eyebreak from neckline to hipline versus a shorter, boxy, widening, waistline break. This also tends to elongate the Body Shape in general, and keeps the eye away from the short Waist.

It is very important to locate the Silhouettes necessary to fulfill your wardrobe needs. Look for longer, leaner black jackets without the front patch pockets. Look for longer and leaner vests and silk button front maxi dresses to be worn as open jacket layers over your trousers/jeans. Look for a longer leaner top with a possible hip belt. Fabric weights are important, as looks are ruined if you have to take off the third layer.

Remember, too, that as a Short-waisted woman, it is not an option to ever tuck anything into the waist of a trouser, skirt, jean or maxi skirt, because doing so cuts you in half into a square box on your top half, making you appear wider, deeper and/or shorter. Find a longer, leaner Silhouette that looks the best and keep it for the rest of your life.

The jackets Short-waisted women should avoid are fitted, belted, and shaped, seamed, semi-fitted, shorter, short, boxy, bulky, in stiff fabrics or light colors. All of these jackets have hemlines that hit close to the waist, and this will make the Short-waisted body visually appear wider, deeper, squarer, larger, and shorter.

Dresses for Short-waisted Women:
The best dress Silhouettes for Short-waisted women are shifts, chemises, sheaths, floats, and dropped waists. Purchase these straight-lined dresses in varying lengths and varying necklines for variety. These cuts are no-waistline dresses and work because they camouflage Waistplacement and create a longer bodyline; therefore, you will appear longer, leaner, taller, narrower, and thinner.

Never select a fitted, belted, seamed dress. Avoid two-toned top and bottom dresses. Different colors at top and bottom whether in a dress or blouse and skirt are the wrong Silhouette, cutting the body in half. Fitted or two-toned at top and bottom dresses will not work on a Short Waist, regardless of weight loss or muscle mass, because even after alterations, they will make you appear boxier, shorter, wider and heavier, no matter what you weigh.

SILHOUETTE SELECTION TIPS FOR LONG-WAISTED WOMEN:

Long-waisted women, regardless of weight or height, have an UNCHANGEABLE WAIST PLACEMENT, and this will mean some Silhouettes will not work on their bodies, but others will. Usually, Long-waisted women are shorter in height have shorter legs and a longer stride, which becomes a challenge for jeans, shorts and trousers. Learning the Silhouettes/styles that work on your Long-waisted Body Shape is essential.

Long-waisted women look DIVINE in all the fitted-at-the-waist, belted-at-the-waist, wrapped-at-the-waists dresses, skirts, jackets, tops, coats, gowns, wedding dresses, and special occasion wear. The challenge is **finding these** to fit your waist position because they are available only in Balanced-waisted.

Long-waisted women may opt to wear no-waist Silhouettes to avoid those fit challenges, selecting silhouettes in chemises, floats, sheaths, and straightlined dresses. Long-waisted women may belt the no-waistline Silhouettes to accent their waists. In fact, belting at the waist becomes a common day-to-day accessory choice. It is ideal to wear a wider belt at the waist because of The Space of the Waist®.

The added space from bustline to waistline creates a canvas to decorate with wide, cinched, layering belts and all varieties of tucked-in-the-waist tops. Tops tucked into trousers and jeans or skirts look great on narrower long-waisted women, even in contrasting colors, because on her, neither bodyline nor waistline needs to be elongated. If you are wider and/or deeper, opt out of contrasting colors and wear same color or monochromatic color schemes. The waist on a longer-waisted woman is an *Asset* on which to focus. If you are wider and/or deeper, cardigan sweaters and jackets may be selected in longer lengths and worn open to feature the waistline *Asset*.

Long-waisted women can wear more varieties of skirts than any other Waistplacement. Long-waisted women can wear an array of short and shorter, novelty-shaped skirts with thicker and stiffer fabrics in their jackets. They can even wear shine.

Jackets for Long-Waisted Women:

Strong shoulders in the jacket are important and are best padded and defined, in arched, squared or curved shapes. The strong shoulder frames the usually longer neck and pronounced collarbone of the Long-waisted woman. The shoulder of the jacket Silhouette sets the tone of the jacket and initiates the long journey from neck to the longer Waistplacement. Highly stylized jacket Silhouettes with a strong shape look very well on long waists, because they help structure and fill the longer top-half of the body, by filling the space between neckline to waistline. The jacket gives any Long-waisted woman a strong presence.

When it comes to teaming these jackets for our daily looks, we generally choose trousers, jeans or skirts, if not a dress. The long-waisted woman usually has shorter legs, so the trousers or jeans are usually best in an easy fit that hangs straight from the hips, a bootcut, or simple flare Silhouette. These Silhouettes will not overwhelm the short legged, shorter bottom half of the body but, at the same time, will balance the top half which carries the longer Waistplacement and added length. Trousers may be in lighter colors and solids as well as smaller prints / patterns, if the Long-waisted woman is taller and slimmer or shorter and narrower. If she is wider and/or deeper, the dark grounded small prints/patterns in Darker Pigments, or solids, work the best.

Jacket Silhouettes that can be teamed with trousers/jeans/skirts are vast: shorter, short, peplums, fitted, semi-fitted, princess seamed, shaped, semi-shaped, boxy, flyaway and geometric shapes of circles, squares, triangles or inverted triangles.

Jackets look stellar in shorter lengths but may be worn in longer lengths. Coats could be fingertip or three-quarter length and, again, in wonderful geometric shapes, and in a wide variety of bolder prints/patterns. The geometric shapes look nice on women who are narrower and taller, or narrower and shorter, as these coats become a canvas, much like Art, to wear. If you are shorter and wider and/or deeper, solid Dark Pigments are the best choices for elongating the bodyline.

Longer shaped and fitted jackets may work fine, if the Long-waisted woman is longer legged or taller. If you are shorter and with shorter legs, jackets, skirtsuits and pantsuits look best when they are all-in-one-color. The key in jacket length for the Long-waisted woman is the proper proportion to legs. Due to the elongation of the legs while wearing stilettos longer jackets and skinnier, narrower trousers, jeans and skirts are worn the most successfully. Higher heels add length to the legs and, therefore, elongate the overall body length and serve to balance a longer jacket length. The top to bottom marriage balance is created through the longer jacket being balanced by legs elongated in higher heels.

The vast array of wonderful highly stylized jackets and strong shouldered Silhouettes for Long-waisted women look amazing when teamed with a wide variety of sweeping shapes in skirts, which are a KEY Classification and are detailed below.

Skirts for Long-waisted Women:
There are multitudes of sweeping skirts that work beautifully on Long-waisted women. Your Waistplacement is designed for many of these, and they are available in an abundance of colors, prints, patterns, softer flowing fabrics, stiffer fabrics, and even heavier fabrics. Skirts in a variety of lengths work for Long-waisted women, especially when selected specifically to balance leg length and overall bodyline. If you are a shorter woman (under 5'4"), proportion is usually best served with lengths right-above-the-knee and right-below-the-knee. Ankle lengths, maxis and full lengths are terrific on most everyone.

Some great skirt Silhouettes for the Long-waisted woman are circle and other Geometrically shaped skirts (square, inverted triangle, triangle or trapeze, and rectangle), fitted and flared, pleated (in a huge variety), trumpeted, tiered, drapes, rouched, ruffled, A-lines, and gathered.

Long-waisted women can enjoy heavily embellished skirt bodies, either self-colored or multi-colored. A host of feminine and decorative hemlines that serve the longer waists well are available.

When Long-waisted, select skirts in a vast variety of color and in large, small and medium-scaled prints, patterns.

Avoid too limp fabrics and too over-scaled or over-sized Silhouettes. Be careful not to confuse strong Silhouettes, strong shoulders and sculptural-shaped silhouettes with over-scaled Silhouettes or over-sized clothing, because the best Silhouettes for the Long-waisted are strong, structured Silhouettes and sculptural designs.

Raglan sleeves, dropped shoulders and weak shoulders do not work well on Long-waisted women. The weak shouldered Silhouettes tend to drag the Long-waisted woman to the ground, and also leave the eye with an undefined Body Shape.

In general, Long-waisted Body Shape tends to get lost, as the eye from neck to waistplacement is so long and because it takes the eye longer to locate the line from neckline to waistline. The neck is usually longer with a pronounced collarbone, the legs are usually shorter, and, at first glance, the Gestalt is already skewed. However, if you add a statement necklace to the strong collarbone on the longer neck, teamed with a strong shoulderline and a printed-all-over jacket in a strong sculptural shape (like a peplum jacket), all of a sudden, you have a Body Shape that is very well defined. Team this jacket with a wonderful crystal (quarter-inch) or knife (half-inch) pleated skirt (half-inch) and a pair of stilettos. Once again, you have movement into a very strong Body Shape that speaks loudly, and with presence.

Dresses for Long-waisted Women:
Terrific, key Silhouettes for Long-waisted women are fitted and flared, princess seamed, belted at the waist, fitted at the waist, semi fitted, A-lines, corseted, wraps and ties, and Geometrically shaped dresses in circles, squares, triangles and rectangle shapes. These Silhouettes look fabulous on Long-waisted women because they have the necessary space from bustline to waistline to accommodate fitted waists and belts, in dress Silhouettes. Due to room in this area of the torso, women with long waists may layer belts, wear wider or cinched belts, and capitalize on flattering and featuring the waist. Especially beautiful on Long-waists are belted and fitted at the waists Silhouettes.

These fitted at the waist Silhouettes allow the top half of the body, with it's actually too-long waist position, to marry well to its (usually) shorter bottom half, including the shorter legs.

Follow the shoulder lines in jackets, for dresses, as the same principles apply. Only a statement necklace can skew the longer neck and pronounced the collarbone. The other options are no-waist dresses or dropped-waist dresses. If you opt for a Dropped-waisted Silhouette in a dress, be certain the skirt body is not flounced, is not big and full, and does not overwhelm the body length from dropped waist to hemline. If you want to wear a fuller skirt, you need the bodyline to be from waist to hemline in order to accommodate that fullness. Otherwise, select straightlined skirt bodies in dropped waists. No-waist dress Silhouettes are available in straighter lines and are better choices.

WHERE ARE OUR CLOTHES?

Men have Longs and Regulars plus free alterations. They receive care in their rises. WHERE are the female Short-waisted and Long-waisted Silhouettes? Women WHERE ARE OUR CLOTHES? Isn't it time to revolutionize The Women's Apparel Industry?

Being forced to conform to a standardized size has encouraged the battle. Standardized sizes used today were developed by the torso dress-form of Haute Couture around 1937. This dress-form was standardized in the 1950's, and was utilized in full force for mass production in the United States by 1960. Some Designers, Vendors and Women's Apparel Manufacturers have adjusted this standardized pattern a tad here and there, but there are still **no LONG-WAISTED OR SHORT-WAISTED** dresses, coats, jackets, suits, tops/sweaters/woven shirtings/blouses, evening gowns, wedding gowns, day dresses, evening dresses, special occasion wear or swimwear available on the market in the proper proportions for these Long and Short-waisted women. Only somewhat-tweaked **Balanced**/Regular-waisted garments are available from the Apparel Industry and Designers as of 2015.

If you have a Regular/**Balanced** Waistplacement, you are lucky, but if you are Longer or Shorter Waisted, you are out of luck. We have been aware and conscious of Waistplacement concerns in sizing for about 50 of the 65 years that sizes have become standardized. **This is just not an intelligent way to offer clothing for women.** Forcing *all women* to conform to a Balanced Waistplacement that facilitates industrialization is very sad. Manufacturing could change if the understanding of WAISTPLACEMENT was integrated AND IMPLEMENTED INTO SIZING. The market should manufacture and offer women size 6S, 6B and 6L (S=SHORT WAIST, B=BALANCED WAIST AND L=LONG WAIST). This book is my first step toward that very goal.

THE BODY SHAPES

In *The Book Series*, all Body Shape information encompasses all heights, widths, and depths. Average height is considered 5'4" and up to 5'10". If 5'10" and over, you would be taller than average. If you are under 5'4", you are considered shorter than average.

The following examples are listed by Body Shape and The Space Of The Waist ®, beginning with Balanced and followed by Short and Long-waisted illustrated examples.

CIRCLE BODY SHAPE: (Books 2, 3, and 4)

The Body Shape is visually rounded, usually due to hips, thighs, buttocks, bust and stomach being fuller in scale. Upon occasion, the buttocks may be flatter or the bustline smaller, but in most cases, all are rounded in visual appearance. Arms and legs are usually in proportion to the body, but some Circles have leaner limbs. What is consistent with Circle Body Shape is that the torso of the body is fuller and rounded in visual appearance.

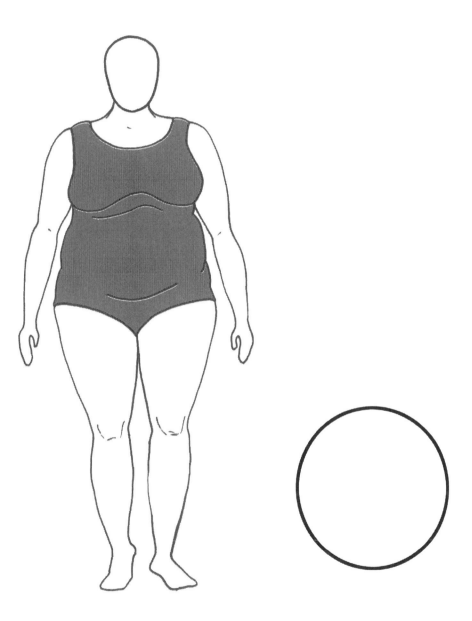

Figure 2 - Circle with a Balanced Waist

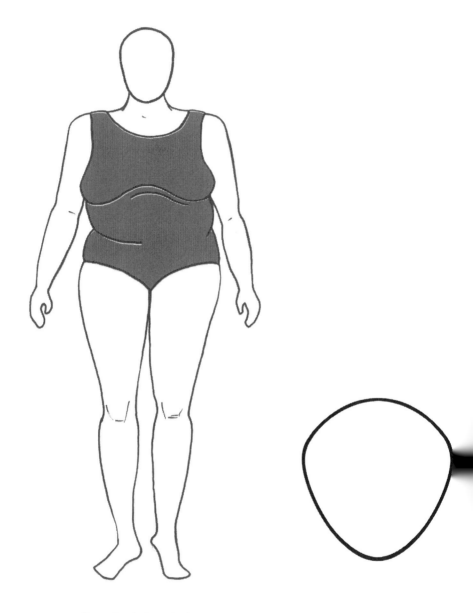

Figure 3 - Circle with Short Waist

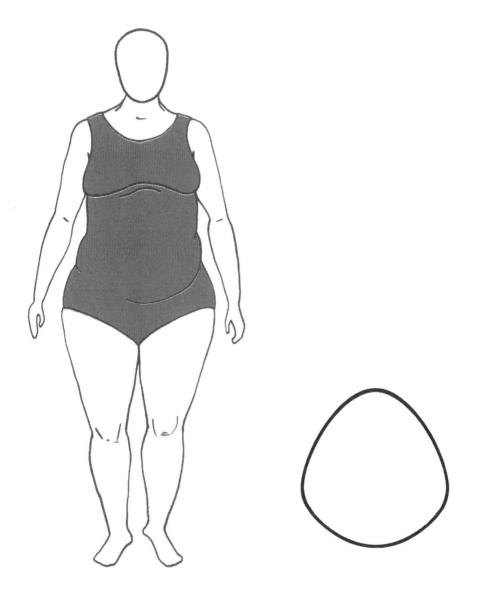

Figure 4 - Circle with Long Waist

SQUARE BODY SHAPE: (Books 5, 6, and 7)

This woman is broader shouldered, broader waisted, with hips about the same width as the shoulders, and always with shorter legs, visually giving a squared appearance. Most Squares have a wider waist but not always. The combination of wider shoulders, the same hips and shoulder width, and short legs formulate the *squared* appearance.

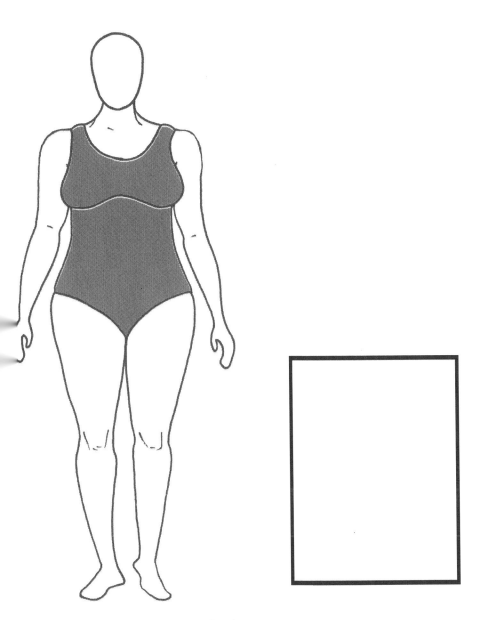

Figure 5 – Square with Balanced Waist

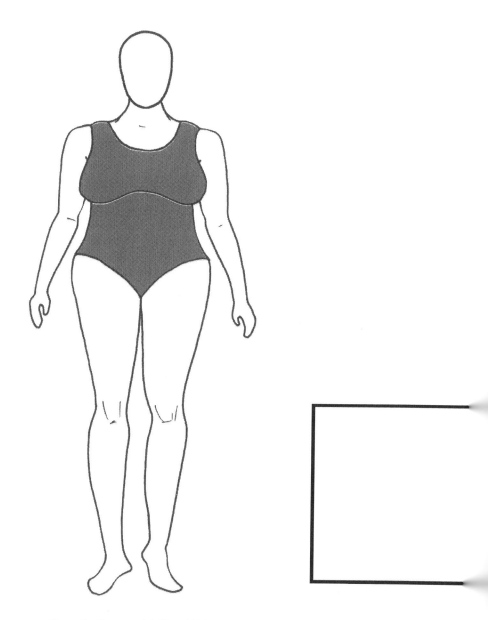

Figure 6 – Square with Short Waist

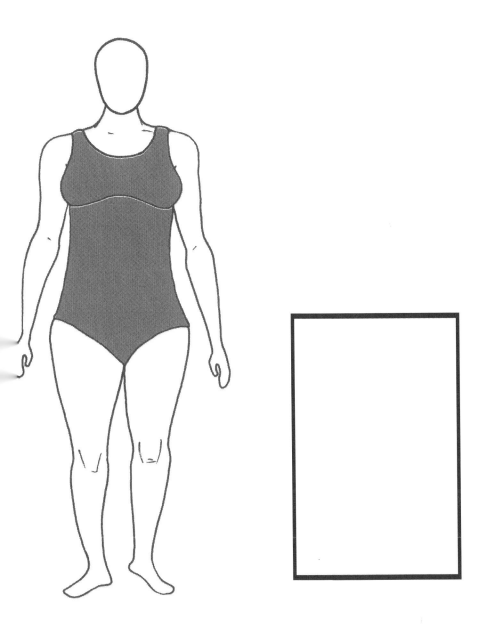

Figure 7 – Square with Long Waist

RECTANGLE BODY SHAPE: (Books 10, 9, and 8)

A woman who has rectangular shape is often referred to as a *ruler,* because her body is nearly without curves, and is straight up and down. The Rectangle Body Shape is built much like a long and lean man or boy. The woman may have real or augmented large breasts, but breast size does not change the fact that hips and shoulders are the same width (or nearly), and that the waist is not 10-inches smaller than her hips. The waistline measurement of a Rectangle is very close to the hip and shoulder widths. Hips, waist, and shoulders appear to be the same widths, thus, linear. Many Rectangles are long and lean. Women with Rectangle shapes appear taller than they actually are. The Rectangle can be wider and/or deeper. Not all Rectangles are narrow.

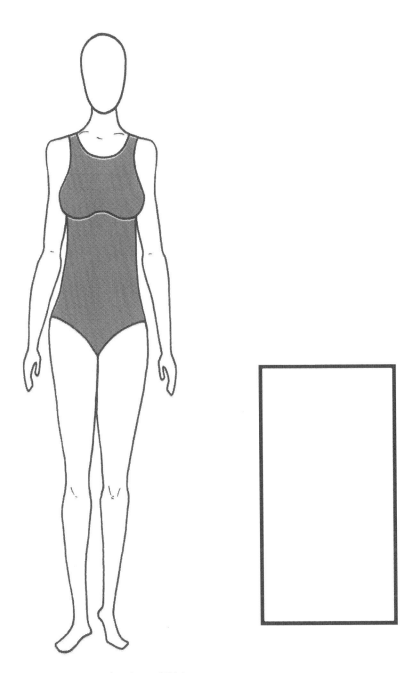

Figure 8 – Rectangle with Balanced Waist

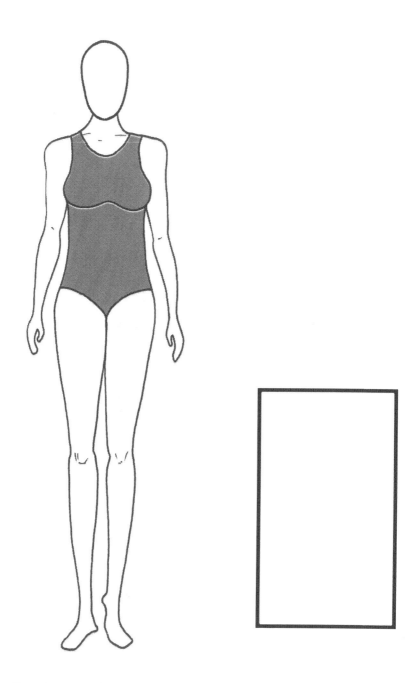

Figure 9 – Rectangle with Short Waist

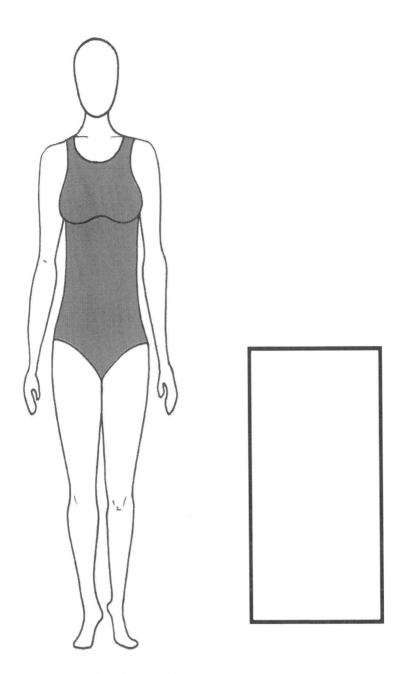

Figure 10 – Rectangle with Long Waist

TRIANGLE BODY SHAPE: (Books 11, 12, and 13)

This shape is created visually due to the shoulders being narrower than the hips. Visually, Triangles resemble the capital letter A. The typical Triangle Body Shape has shoulders that are much narrower than the hips or thigh-hip. The bottom half of the Body Shape is larger than the top half. Sometimes, if you are a Borderliner, a simple addition of shoulder pads creates an Hourglass. Sometimes the shape of the top half is very different than the bottom half. For example, the top half may appear frail, delicate and narrow with an ample bustline, while the bottom half appears extremely muscular, deeper and wider.

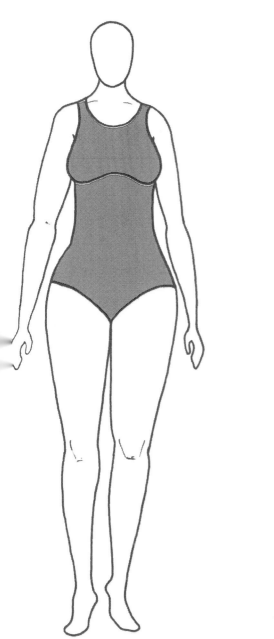

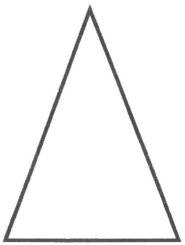

ure 11 – Triangle with Balanced Waist

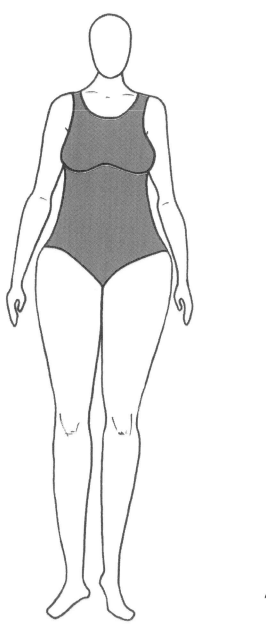

Figure 12 – Triangle with Short Waist

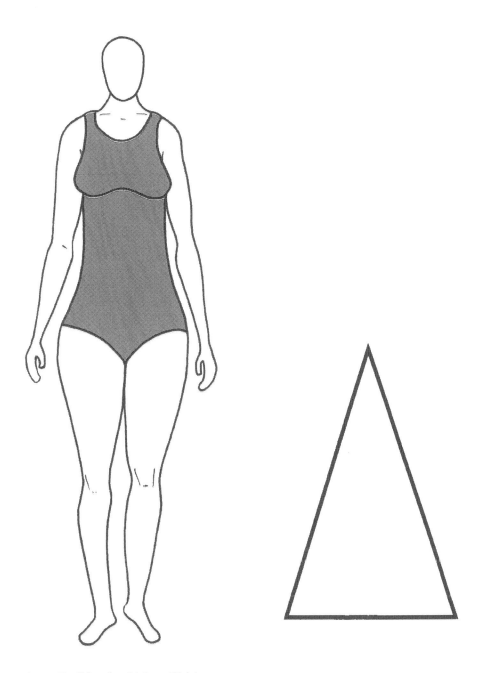

Figure 13 – Triangle with Long Waist

INVERTED TRIANGLE BODY SHAPE: (Books 14, 15, and 16)

This shape is indicated by shoulders that are wider than the hips. Shoulders are wide and pronounced, and hips are narrow; often, but not always, the waist is near the size of the hips. An Inverted Triangle could have a waistline that measures 3 to 10-inches smaller than the hip. The wider shoulder, narrow hip appearance is the criteria to be considered in an Inverted Triangle Body Shape. Usually, Inverted Triangle Shapes have a smaller buttocks and a not-too-narrow waistline and are straightlined versus curved.

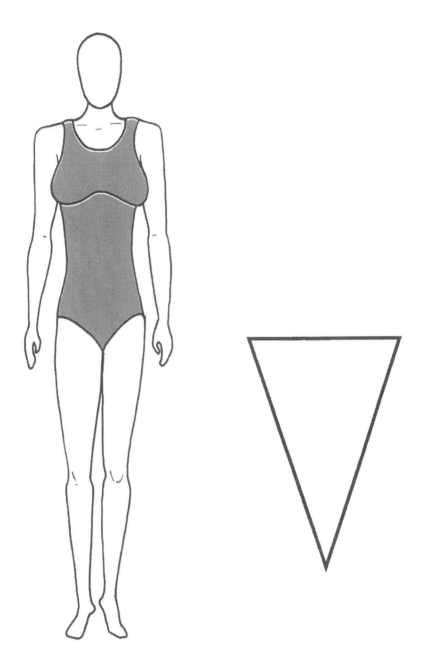

Figure 14 – Inverted Triangle with Balanced Waist

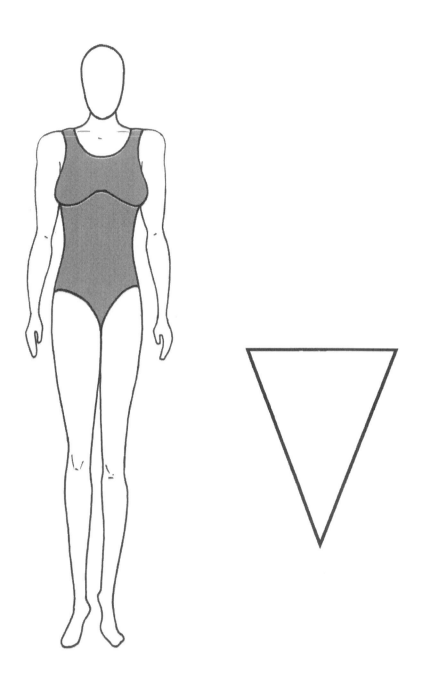

Figure 15 – Inverted Triangle with Short Waist

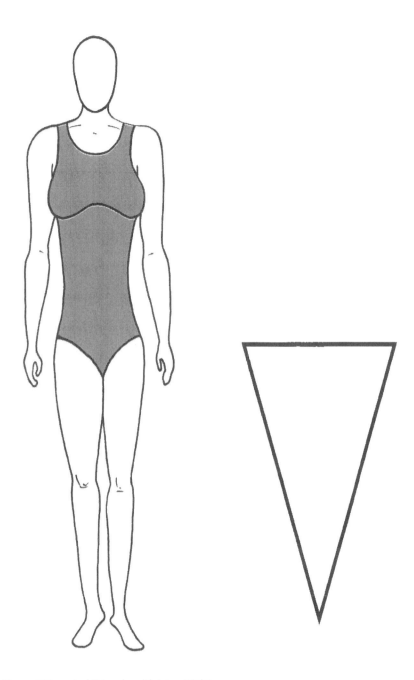

Figure 16 Inverted Triangle with Long Waist

HOURGLASS BODY SHAPE: (Books 17, 18, and 19)

The Hourglass has often been considered the "Ideal" female Body Shape because the proportion is alanced. The ratio is visually pleasing to many because the hips and the shoulders are about the same measurement, and the waist is at least 10-inches smaller in the Iconic Hourglass Body Shape. The Natural hips and shoulders serve as a *frame* accommodating the smaller waistline. Today many Hourglasses are of lower BMI and, therefore, are not as large in the bustline or buttocks as the Iconic Hourglass, but, nonetheless, those with lower BMI are still Hourglasses.

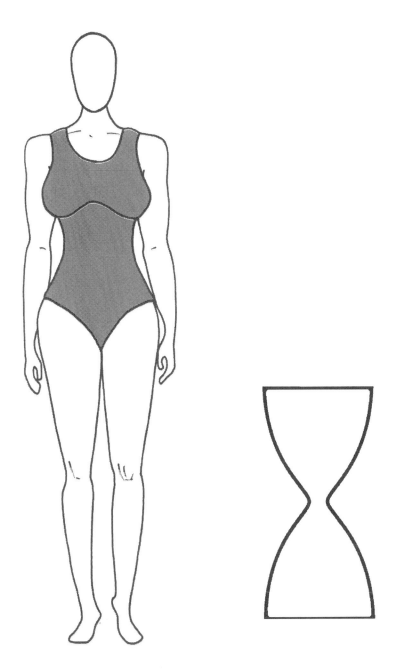

Figure 17 – Hourglass with Balanced Waist

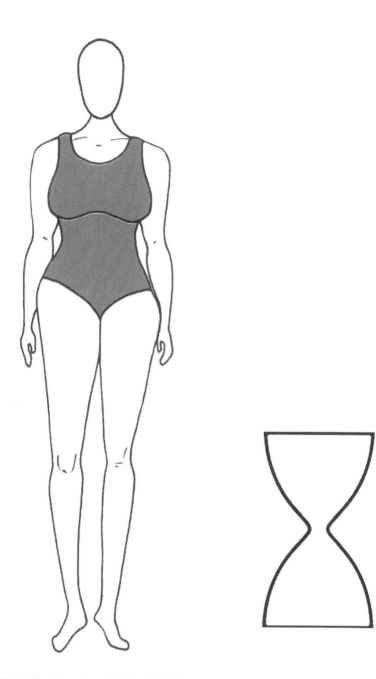

Figure 18 – Hourglass with Short Waist

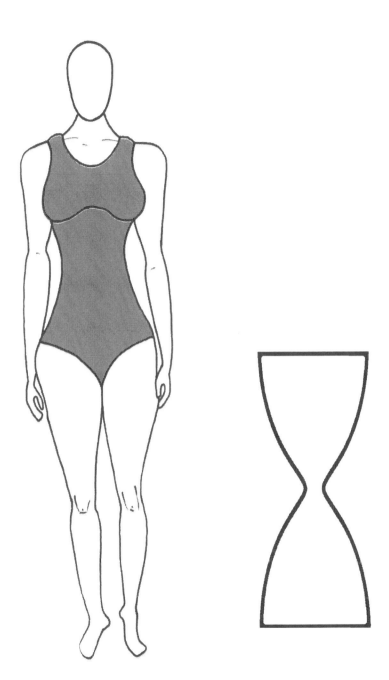

Figure 19 – Hourglass with Long Waist

HOW TO MEASURE IN ORDER TO DETERMINE YOUR INDIVIDUAL BODY SHAPE

To determine your BODY SHAPE, review the measurements areas below.

When measuring, **do not include the buttocks in the hip measurement**. Take the front hip measurement -- left side to right side only -- and double that number. The waist width may be calculated by the same method. **Do not use the buttocks in the hip measurement as it will skew the number** to a larger number, and will not provide the information needed for determining Body Shape/Frame, for the purposes of these books. The Frame/Body Shape is your true width of shoulder, hip and waist. For example, someone may appear to be an Hourglass, but if she takes her measurements including her buttocks, she will become a Triangle; but if her hip frontal view is the same width as her shoulder frontal view, she is Hourglass in Frame.

The location of the Waistplacement and its measurement technique, SPACE OF THE WAIST®, while it is provided through illustration it is measured from right under the breast at the bra band to the nipped-in part of the waist. Please wear your best-uplifting bra when measuring.

* Measure (as indicated in Figure 20) the shoulders, waist and hips for all Body Shapes and include also for Circle Body Shapes, the bustline, abdomen, and high and low hips.

The key measurements for Body Shape are shoulders, waist and hips. You need to measure your height in order to know if you are average, petite, or tall. 5'4" up to 5'11" is considered average height, if your height is under 5'4" you are considered short and may shop in Petite's. If you are over 5'10" you are considered tall and would most likely shop in Tall's. As it relates to sizing in retail, height and proportion are provided through various department types mostly referred to as Regular Misses, Petite Misses, or Tall Misses. (Larger sized women may, yet not always, fall into Plus Sized departments.) Later you will see that the Balanced, Short, or Long waist indicates that THE SPACE OF THE WAIST® is at different lengths for average, petite, and tall women. Keep your measurements handy at all times in your purse or phone for references. After you determine your stride and skirt length preferences, include these in your file as well.

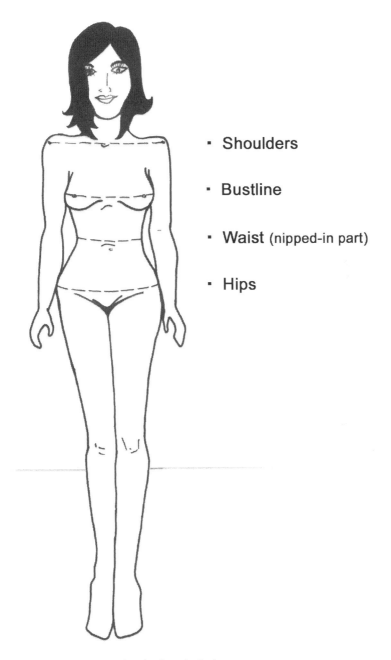

- Shoulders

- Bustline

- Waist (nipped-in part)

- Hips

Figure 20 - Measuring the Female Body

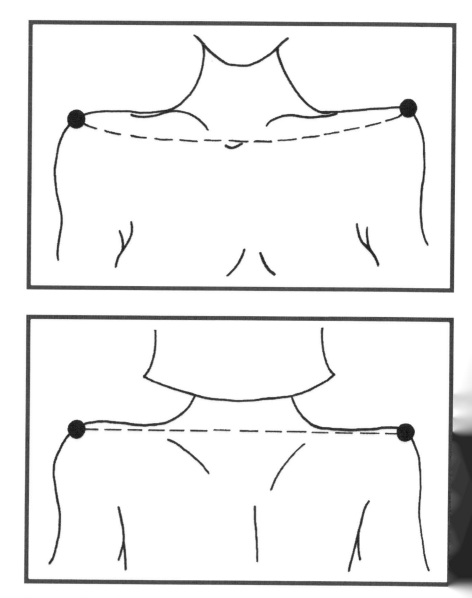

Figure 21 – Measuring Shoulders (front and back)

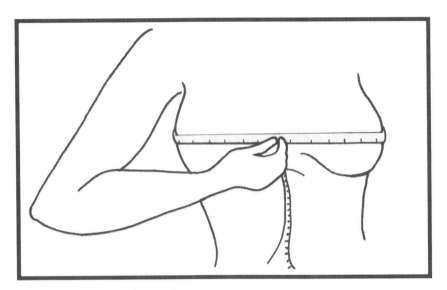

Figure 22 – Measuring the Bust (360°)

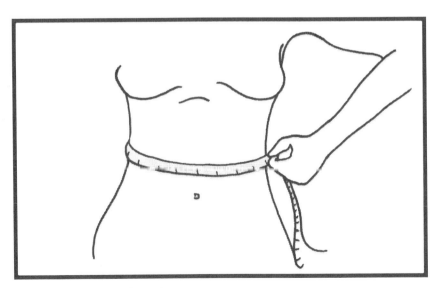

Figure 23 – Measuring the Waist

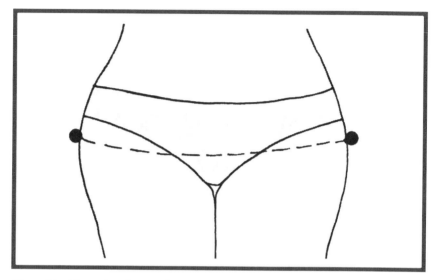

Figure 24 – Measuring the Hips (front view)

THE "CATCHES"

Catches that skew measurements are buttocks size and neck length.
Leave the buttocks out of your measurements and use an average neck
length if your neck is long (or half your neck length); otherwise, the
measurements are not accurate for Body Shape and Waistplacement.
These are the reasons so many measuring methods do not give the True
Body Shape.

THE SPACE OF THE WAIST®

It is essential to determine Waistplacement. It may be Balanced, Short or Long. Waistplacement may be extremely short or long, or just a little off in placement. You must measure to determine your Waistplacement as it is the foundation for the intelligent selection of attractive clothing Silhouettes for you. When you have determined your Waistplacement as either Balanced, Short or Long, you will have also determined **THE SPACE OF THE WAIST**®.

Women become confused when it comes to Waistplacement, and even more confused when they try to factor their **Waistplacement with their particular Body Shape.** It is more common than you would think. A size on a garment does not provide enough information to clothe yourself properly because it does not consider Waistplacement. The sizes offered today are limited to the Balanced Waistplacements. Yet the Waistplacement determines the Silhouette that flatters a woman's body. Not every Silhouette is the right one for every Body Shape and every Waistplacement.

Waistplacement determines the Silhouettes that will flatter the Body Shape. Waistplacement provides the MOST IMPORTANT INFORMATION necessary in determining the **BEST SILHOUETTES** that a woman may **wear successfully**. Body Shape and Waistplacement may be accented and flattered by *selecting* the proper **SILHOUETTES.** The **selection of Silhouettes** is a **skill,** and it is **THE KEY** to **dressing successfully.** The best Silhouettes for your Body Shape with your particular Waistplacement are provided in *The Book Series*. The best selections in Silhouettes best flatter your overall body and proportion.

Focusing your shopping on Silhouettes that are appropriate quickens the process. You will soon discover that *some* Silhouettes will **never** be attractive on your Waistplacement, so those Silhouettes are just a complete "NO WAY EVER FOR ME TO WEAR", moving forward with Silhouettes that *are* attractive on your Body Shape with your Waistplacement. Knowledge and information will make your shopping much quicker, enjoyable and effortless due to this elimination process.

The KEY *knowledge* to obtain in dressing successfully is **KNOWING** *what the parameters are. What are my* **UNCHANGEABLES**?

Throughout *The Book Series*, the term **SILHOUETTE** is used to refer to the distinct styling, cut, fit, shape, length and holistic sum of all details of the garment, as an individual manifestation of style. This sum total is referred to as *the Silhouette*. A few Silhouette examples are: Shirtwaist (dress), fitted and flared (skirt/dress/coat), chemise (dress), shift (dress), reefer coat, puffer coat, peplum jacket, bomber jacket, tunic and crystal pleated skirt. Many **Silhouettes** just fall out of the way for *your* selection once you know your Shape and **Waistplacement. The Shopping List/Recap** at the end of each book in *The Book Series* makes the journey very easy, as all of the wrong Silhouettes are omitted.

HOW TO MEASURE FOR THE SPACE OF THE WAIST®

The Easy Measure Waistplacement (EMWP):

I have provided a simple method: "The Easy Measure Waistplacement" or EMWP. To determine your Waistplacement, measure from right at the bottom of your bra band to the smallest nipped-in place of the waist (See the illustration below on the EMWP measurement technique).

On an average woman of 5 feet 4 inches through 5 feet 10 inches:
* **NOTE:** Measurement Conversion .3 = 5/16 inch.
> Patternmakers usually grade 1/6" to 1/8" from size 8 up or down the sizes.

- A Balanced Waistplacement measurement is 6.3 to 7 inches.
- A Long Waistplacement is any measurement over 7 inches.
- A Short Waistplacement is any measurement under 6.3 inches.

If you are under 5 feet 4 inches tall, your numbers are nearer to 4.3 inches to 5 inches for Balanced Waistplacement; therefore, if you are under these numbers you are Short-waisted. If you are over these numbers, then you are Long-waisted.

If you are over 5 feet 10 inches in height, Balanced Waist Measurement becomes 8.3 to 9 inches. If your measurement is shorter, you are Short-waisted. If your measurement is longer, you are Long-waisted.

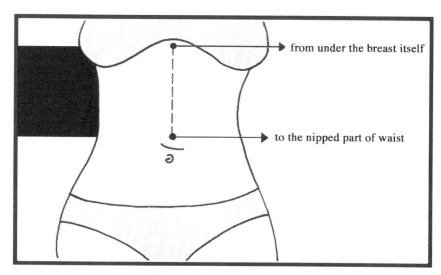

from under the breast itself

to the nipped part of waist

Figure 25 – Measuring area for Waist Placement (EMWP)

EMWP is the preferred and most accurate method to answer questions like: What Silhouettes can I wear successfully? EMWP teaches you THE SPACE OF THE WAIST®.

Determining your Waistplacement helps you determine where and whether you can wear a belt, or if you can wear a fitted-at-the-waist Silhouette at all. Do you have room to wear a wide, thin or medium belt at the waist? Do you know whether your Waistplacement looks good with a low-slung belt at your hips, or if it is better to wear no belt at all? If through taking the EMWP measurement you determine you have under 6.3 inches in THE SPACE OF THE WAIST®, then you are **Short-waisted.** You will never, ever be able to wear those earlier mentioned belted, fitted at the waist, or hemlines that hit at the waist (like short fitted jackets), because you will look wider, shorter, deeper, or boxier, basically more squared, regardless of your Body Shape. The waistlines of all jackets you try on in the stores today, when you are Short-waisted, will hit you lengthwise more closely to **your hip,** the **widest** part of your body. This is why straightlined jackets are the best. Also, you may have higher hips as many Short-waisted women do, and this accentuates and increases that visual of the wider look at the hips. Longer, below the hip and straightlined jackets are your answer. Knits work the easiest.

If you have more than 6.3 to 7 inches of space from the bottom of the bra-band to the nipped in waist, you are **Long-waisted.** For the Long-waisted woman, dresses on the market today with fitted waists will nip in *above* your Natural-waistline. What a shame, you would wear them beautifully if they were simply cut to your Longer Waistplacement.

Determining your Waistplacement eliminates trying on *inappropriate Silhouettes*. EMWP, in my opinion, is the overall best method for measuring because it is fast, easy, accurate and uncomplicated. However, I provide an overview of other methods for measuring. Below, are illustrations to further explain the Balanced (B), Short (S), and Long (L) Waistplacements positioned on the torso.

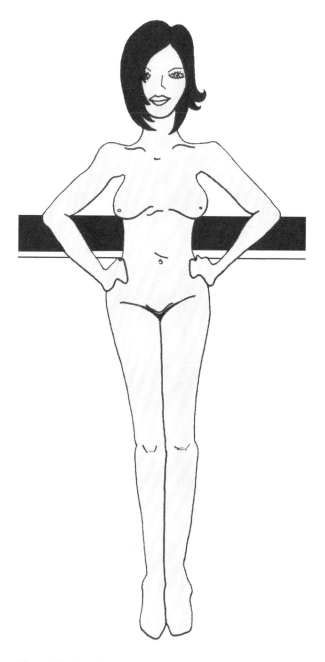

Figure 26 – Female Figure with Balanced Waist Placement

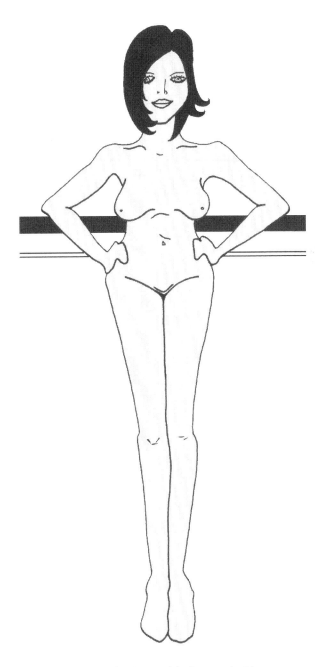

Figure 27 – Female Figure with Short Waist Placement

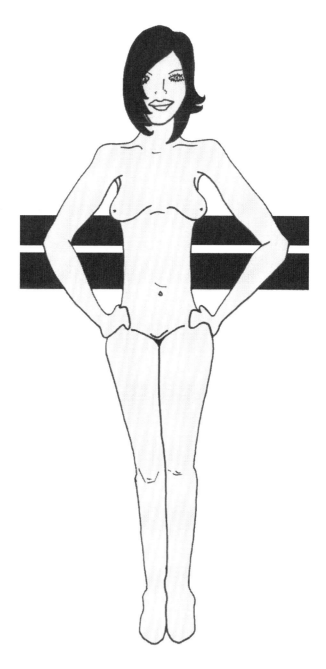

Figure 28 – Female Figure with Long Waist Placement

OTHER METHODS FOR MEASURING WAISTPLACEMENT

Two-Hands Method: Hold your own two hands (one on top of the other) under the bust-line to see if these two hands fit in the space between bust and nipped-in waist. If you can insert your 2-hands, you are Balanced-waisted. If there is space left over, you are Long-waisted. If the hands do not fit and only one hand and part of another hand fit, you are Short-waisted. I'm not happy with this method because women's hands come in varying sizes, so this method does not always read true.

Hip to Tip-Top Method: Another method is measuring from the hip line to the tip of your breast. Then measure the tip of your breast to the top of your head. If your hip to breast measurement is less than your breast to head measurement, you are Short-waisted. I do not really like this method because it includes the neck length, which can influence the measurement by several inches. If you have a long neck, you will measure longer from the breast to the top of head. This measurement method does not provide clarity in terms of knowing if you have THE SPACE OF THE WAIST®.

Total Height Method: Measure your total height from the head to the toe. Now measure from your toes to the widest part of your hip. Determine where your hip is in relation to your total height. If your hip is halfway up your body, it is balanced. Example: If your height is 5 feet 10 inches -- or 70 inches -- and your hips are 35 inches (toes to wide hip), you are Balanced Waistplacement. If the top half measurement is larger than the bottom half measurement, you are Long-waisted. If the top half is shorter than the bottom, you are considered Short-waisted. Because this measurement includes the neck, again, I find it does not produce an accurate measure when the neck is longer.

Ribs and Hips: Measure the distance between your bottom rib and the top of your hipbone. You are 25/75 type if the distance is 1 to 2-inches, which means you are Short-waisted. This means your upper torso is 25% of total body with 75% being lower body (from where your leg bends to sit and below). You are 50/50 body type if the distance is about 2 to 3-inches, which means you are balanced with your waist coming around the midpoint of your total body length. This method is not accurate because it does not allow you to discover THE SPACE OF THE WAIST®, or the number of inches between the bottom of the bustline/bra band to the nipped-in part of the waist.

Armpit to Waist: Measure the distance between your armpit and your waist. Then, measure the distance between your waist to the bottom of your buttocks. If the two measurements aren't equal, you are Short or Long-waisted. If the first measurement is shorter, you are Short-waisted. If the second measurement is shorter, you are Long-waisted. This is not a viable measuring method because it does not take into consideration the bustline placement and the inches available between bust and waist.

Head to Floor Method: Measure from top of the head to nipped in waist. Measure nipped-in waist to the floor. You are Short-waisted if the top half of the body is shorter than the bottom half of the body. This measuring method is not accurate, due to a *long* neck length will skew the number on top.

The Golden Ratio: To fully understand a numerical measurement, the Golden Ratio, which is important to visual Gestalt, must be considered. What one may define as attractiveness is simply a matter of mathematical symmetry. The mathematical process is the Golden Ratio. The Golden Ratio seems to define what proportions look visually appealing for example, with the length of the arms and legs compared to the torso. In mathematical terms, **the GOLDEN RATIO IS A COMPARISON OF TWO ASPECTS THAT UNDERLIES PROPORTION BECOMING VIEWED IN AN IDEAL WAY.** According to the Golden Ratio, if you have 2 numbers, A and B, then: A + B / A = B. Usually this is the ratio of 1 to 1.618.

The Easy Measure Waistplacement or EMWP is the simple 6.3 to 7-inch method and serves as a holistic visual Gestalt for THE SPACE OF THE WAIST®, considering the Golden Ratio.

WHAT'S TORSO GOT TO DO WITH WAISTPLACEMENT?

Waistplacement is located on the torso of the body. The torso itself can be long or short in length. Waistplacement has nothing to do with the length of the torso. Waistplacement has to do with where the waist resides *on* the torso (See following illustrations: Figures 29, 30, 31, and 32). The waist could be a short or a long placement.

In average height women, a woman with only 3-inches of space from under the bottom of the bra band to the nipped-in part of the waist would be considered Short-waisted. These women have the dilemma of not having much space to work with in THE SPACE OF THE WAIST®. If the female has a short torso and is average height, as for example 5'5", yet has 8.4 inches from under the bustline to the nipped-in part of the waist, she would be considered Long-waisted.

For shorter or taller than average height, the concept is the same (refer to page 68 for waist length measurements).

If an individual is an uncommon denominator, adjust accordingly. For instance, Shorter Waists tend to have longer legs and shorter strides. Longer Waists tend to have shorter legs and longer strides.

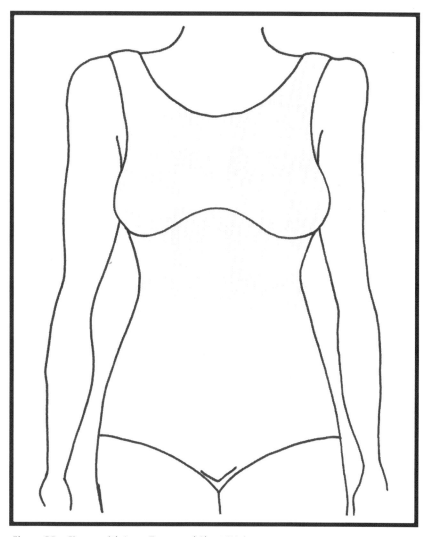

Figure 29 – Figure with Long Torso and Short Waist

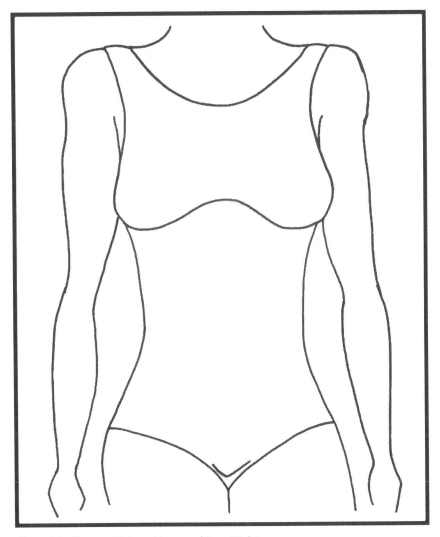

Figure 30 – Figure with Long Torso and Long Waist

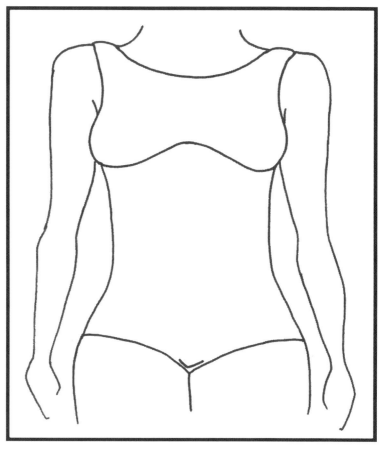

Figure 31 – Figure with Short Torso and Long Waist

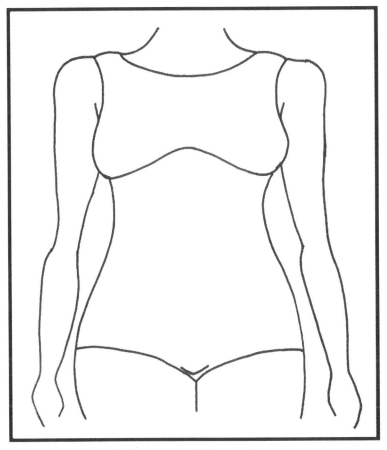

Figure 32 – Figure with Short Torso and Short Waist

WHAT'S STRIDE GOT TO DO WITH FIT?

Stride is a Secondary Modifier. Stride is the crotch length, the length from waist to crotch. Stride affects the fit of your trousers. Just as you may have a Balanced, Short, or Long Waistplacements, you may have a Balanced, Short or Long Stride; however, Stride and Waistplacement are very different (See illustrations below: Figures 33, 34, 35, and 36).

As far as strides go, Longer Waisted women usually have longer strides and shorter legs. The Short Waists usually have shorter strides and longer legs. There are some who fall outside of these norms.

Strides confuse women, as trousers are often too long or too short in the crotch. Short-waisted women usually find themselves in the fitting room with too much fabric in the crotch. Long-waisted women have too little length in the crotch, causing trousers or jeans to get wrinkles and folds across the pelvic area. On long strides, trousers usually cut in the crotch and are extremely uncomfortable. All trousers are not created equally. It is helpful to search the marketplace for the Brands/Labels and Designers that best fit your Body Proportion and Stride. If the Stride is too short or too long, a seamstress must make the proper alterations. Knowing how to determine your Stride and knowing if you have a Balanced, Short or Long-Stride will help you to understand your trouser stride challenges.

Determine your stride by measuring from front to back from the middle of your Natural-waistline by running a tape measure between your legs and through your crotch (See Figure 33). It is best to have a terrific seamstress adjust your trousers or jeans to fit your own body. Seldom is any woman naturally a size off the rack.

When giving measurements to a tailor versus a seamstress, please clarify STRIDE from RISE. State you are describing **STRIDE** -- not rise. Rise is a very different number and method of measurement that men use.

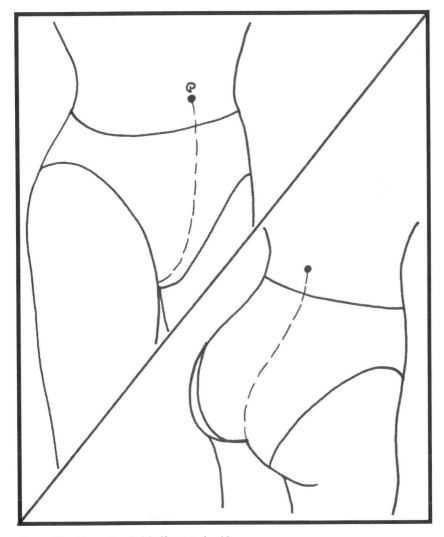

Figure 33 – Measuring Stride (front to back)

The Formulas for Strides:

Balance= B/s

Short=S/s

Long=L/s

Stride versus Rise: Rise is used most often to mean the measurement from the Natural-waist to the crotch. This is not the same number women need to use for issues relating to Stride. It is important to explain to your seamstress **how you have arrived at the measurement for Stride,** measuring from the front of the Natural-Waistband, under the crotch to the back of the Natural-Waistband of your trouser. *SOME* seamstresses refer to Stride as the shorter number of waist to crotch alone, and that would be **incorrect.**

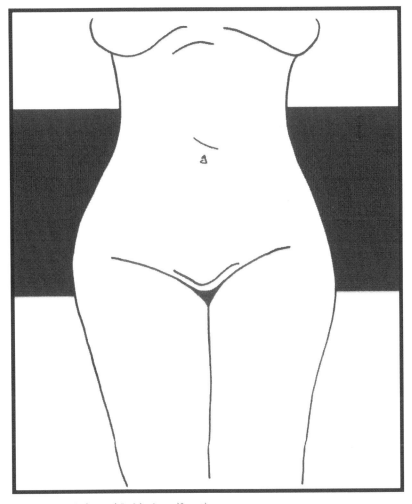

Figure 34 – Balanced Stride Area (front)

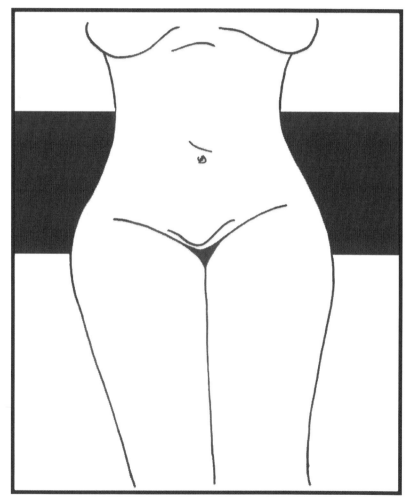

Figure 35 – Short Stride Area (front)

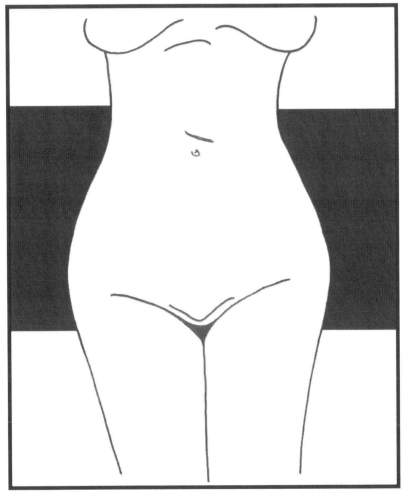

Figure 36 – Long Stride Area (front)

WHAT ARE YOUR ASSETS?

I like to think of *Assets* as those unique-to-the-self attributes of both inner qualities and outer/visible ones. *Assets* may include vibrational feeling, personality, inner-essence, sense of humor, attitude, and sensitivity, along with your most visible attractive features such as face, eyes, hair texture, hair color, hair style, hands, neck, bustline, abdominal area, waistline, legs, ankles, feet, arms, hands, fingers or skin quality or color. Explore these listed and add your many more. The idea is to embrace and reveal the **Assets** you choose when you desire. When selecting your clothing and looks, it is always best to take into consideration your individual *Assets.*

Assets are your unique qualities in personal attributes. The *Assets* to focus upon at any given time may be physical features considered attractive. There may be more subtle aspects or qualities to feature in either a bold or subtle manner. The key is filtering the *Assets* into your looks and into the selection of your Silhouette choices.

These Secondary Modifiers are listed here lastly, simply because they do not affect **fit**. But *ASSETS* are certainly considerations in apparel, as you want to dress in Silhouettes and create looks that feel *authentic*. But everyone needs to be a "Rock Star, a "Glamour Queen" or an artsy woman once a year! You should not forget your own *unique* personal *Assets* when selecting Silhouettes and deciding upon looks to include in your wardrobe.

I feel *Assets* should be exploited because they are unique gifts. You can choose to hide them or display them. Some Assets are listed below as a guide, yet the list is not all-inclusive. A complete list could be endless. A woman may desire to feature an *ASSET* from time to time but not every day. For example, you may want to feature your femininity, sexiness, and your minimalistic Nature, your belief in planetary salvation and GREEN mindset. Other features to focus on could be your beautiful physical features of beauty such as your face, skin, eyes, neck or hair.

SOME *ASSETS* YOU MAY WISH TO FEATURE:

Outer *Assets:* Face, Smile, Eyes, Teeth, Skin, High Cheekbones, Nose, Lips, Hair (Shine, length, color, style), Hands, Knees, Legs, Ankles, Arms, Neck, Shoulders, Body Shape, Frame, Bustline, Buttocks, Waistline, Flat Stomach, Proportion, Focus of Fashion Trend, Love and Interests, Favorite Color Display, Posture, Carriage, Body Language

Inner *Assets*: (to reveal on the outside)
Tenderness, Intelligence, Planetary Love, Animal Love, People Love, Soft Gentle Nature, Humility, Humbleness, Shyness, Strength, Courage, Risk Taker Persona, Loud Gutsy Nature, Quieter Inter-perspective Self, Personality, Inner Self, Sense of Humor, Intention, Profession, Musical Love, Scientific Interest, Quantum Physics Interest, Spirituality, Religious Nature, Holistic Approach to Life, Love for Speed or Racing, Gardening, Flower and Plant Love, Insect Love, Bird Love, Reptile Love, Tree love, Mountain Love, Seaside Love, Various Planetary Signs to Display, Folkloric Loves, UFO Knowledge, Experience and Belief, Professional Attributes, Honors and Rewards, Image to Project, Self- Acceptance, Self-Assurance, Self-Confidence, Patience, Positive Attitude, Interest and Curiosity, Vitality

You will see how knowledge about Stride, Fit, and *Assets* will begin to make personal Silhouette selections far easier. Shopping will be fun and not take nearly as long, or create as many nightmare scenes in the dressing rooms of retail stores across the globe. Once the Waistplacement is known and integrated with Stride, Fit, and Assets, a Gestalt is produced while creating looks, and, instantly, you will recognize that your look is both immediately attractive and pleasing, or it is not and you need to select another.

FORMULAS FOR LINE/EYEBREAKS: CREATING WITH LAYERS OF CLOTHING

Using eyebreaks is a method of layering to make the appearance of the body more visually pleasing. Eyebreaks can be utilized to make the body appear longer and leaner, to move the eye away from featuring the waist, broader shoulders, or to create more curves. Layering can change the width of the shoulders if they are narrow, or diminish the appearance of wider shoulders. Eyebreaks can create visually narrower or broader hips. Layering is common in women for creating looks and can be executed wisely in order to flatter a particular Waistplacement and Body Shape.

Included is a brief explanation of the **FORMULAS**. Examples are provided in *The Book Series* for your individual Body Shape and Waistplacement. The FORMULAS will be expressed *mostly* through clothing layers creating eyebreaks on the Body. Formulas are presented in the following layers of 4, 3, 2, or 1 layer/s or eyebreaks. Layers that are created through this method flatter the body through the visual creation of line breaks. (Sometimes an eyebreak can be as simple as a white collar popping out of a black sweater, but usually they are created through hemlines of individual garments when layered.

Eyebreaks allow the eye to follow the lines created, most often, through layers of clothing. The lines or layers may be created in 4, 3, or 2 lines as you layer garments to create your looks or wear 1 piece like a dress.

Illustrations, written guides, and **Formulas** throughout *The Book Series* are to aid in selecting appropriate and successful Silhouettes for your unique Body Shape and Waistplacement. With this knowledge, you may begin later, on your own, to utilize accessories, select a *Shape-Shifter,* or use shawl or scarf as a visual break. But for the purpose of *The Book Series* Books 2-19 by Body Shape by Waistplacement, Silhouette hemlines will *most-often* be utilized to create these lines/eyebreaks.

FOUR LINE/EYE BREAKS:

Four breaks may be created by selecting clothing as layers. They may also be created with color, or details like fishtails on hemlines, longer coattails or trains on dresses. For example, a long black coat to the ankle creates line one; a navy skirt to the mid-calf hemline in a trumpeted Silhouette creates line two; line three is a burgundy blouse to the hip, and the fourth line is created with a short shrug to a length right under the breasts. Through garment length, 4 visual eyebreaks have been created. This is the process of layering and creating lines for eyebreaks. Looks listed and detailed in the individual books describe best how to flatter the featured Body Shape and Waistplacement.

*** See Figure 37, FOR ANOTHER LOOK.

Figure 37 – Example Outfit: Four Line Breaks

THREE LINE/EYE BREAKS:

Three breaks may be created by clothing, color or details such as tailcoat length and high/low lengths. Three distinct lines on the body can be created through a tight, dark-navy skinny jean hemline length, a long white tunic hemline and a short light pink fitted jacket.

*** See Figure 38, FOR ANOTHER LOOK.

Figure 38 – Example Outfit: Three Line Breaks

TWO LINE/EYE BREAKS:

Two breaks may be created by clothing, color or details. A navy-blue jacket and a white trouser create two visual breaks.

*** See Figure 39, FOR ANOTHER LOOK.

Figure 39 – Example Outfit: Two Line Breaks

ONE LINE/EYE BREAKS:

One break is a 1-piece garment in a solid color or an allover print. **One hemline** on the body, and ONLY one hemline, creates the key eyebreak or line I; for example, a shift dress in navy, a jumpsuit with no waist in solid black, or a steamer coat in a camel color. There is no line break in the garment; it is **ONE LINE.**

*** See Figure 40, FOR ANOTHER LOOK.

Figure 40 – Example Outfit: One Line, no breaks

BODY SHAPES BY WAISTPLACEMENT IN THE FORMULAS

Explained and illustrated in detail below are the six Body Shapes of Circle, Square, Rectangle, Triangle, Inverted Triangle and Hourglass and their Waist Symbols of B, S, L (Balanced-waist, Short-waist and Long-waist). Also included are the created eyebreaks through the use of Silhouette layers, layering techniques, or lines used to break the Body Shape into 4, 3, 2, or 1 line/s. The numbers for the Formulas 4, 3, 2, and 1 indicate layers or lines created and their resulting eyebreaks. The eye breaks when the hemlines, details or color pops. The eyebreaks are important to plan and learn as a skill, to best flatter your Body Shape and Waistplacement. The eye grazes the figure of a woman and stops if the layer is too contrasting or overly embellished in any specific area. The eye flows the *most* linearly through all-in-one dark colors, or through the use of monochromatic colors in the same color scheme. These breaks may be used to your advantage or disadvantage. Select eyebreaks wisely.

One-line division is expressed as Formula 1, and may be any single item that has one line break: the Silhouette of a shift dress in a solid color or a solid colored coat. For an example of 2 line breaks or Formula 2, consider either: a jacket and a skirt, a jacket and a trouser, or a black and white dress with a white bodice and a black flared skirt, creating 2 lines. A short bright colored jacket, a longer top in a lighter color, and a long lean skirt to below the knee in black create 3 lines or Formula 3. For 4 lines or layers or Formula 4, consider a long coat to the ankle, layered over a mid-calf lean skirt worn with a hip-length top and another light weight sweater hitting at below the bustline, creating 4 distinct lines that are also 4 distinct layers.

Symbolized as follows are the Formulas (4, 3, 2, 1) for the layer, lines or eye breaks by Body Shape and the Waistplacement of B = Balanced-waisted, S = Short-waisted or L = Long-waisted. All of the 6 Body Shapes -- Circle, Square, Rectangle, Triangle, Inverted Triangle and Hourglass -- have 3 Waistplacements B, S or L as their Primary Modifiers. You are ONE Body Shape and ONE WAISTPLACEMENT and have ONE BOOK in the series of 18 to download/purchase.

One of the Body Shapes is a Circle. If you are a Circle and have a Balanced Waistplacement then you should download/purchase Circle B. You will be provided with examples to improve your layering in order to flatter your Body Shape with its particular Waistplacement, through the eyebreaks of 4, 3, 2 or 1 line/s.

Directly below are the Balanced, Short and Long-waisted Formulas to be used with each of the Body Shapes. For clarity, below this you will find each Body Shape and the Waistplacements identified individually. There are 18 possibilities in total. Find the one that identifies your individual (one) Body Shape and (one) Waistplacement and download/purchase your book. I encourage you to keep it in your handbag for shopping trips and accidental finds.

Formula B for Balanced-Waisted = B4, B3, B2, and B1

Formula S for Short-Waisted = S4, S3, S2, and S1

Formula L for Long-Waisted = L4, 3, L2, and L1

WAISTPLACEMENT FORMULAS APPLIED TO THE BODY SHAPES

Three ensembles are provided in dialogue form, as well one additional illustrated example, of looks in each of the layering techniques of either 4, 3, 2, or 1 layer(s) in *The Book Series* for each of the Individual Body Shapes for each Waistplacement.

THE COMPLETE LIST OF THE EYEBREAKS/LAYERS FORMULAS BY BODY SHAPE AND THEIR INDIVIDUAL WAISTPLACEMENT ARE AS FOLLOWS.

CIRCLE BALANCED WAIST = CIRCLE B: in 4, 3, 2 or 1 line/eyebreak(s). FORMULAS FOR CIRCLE B BELOW:
Circle B4
Circle B3
Circle B2
Circle B1

CIRCLE SHORT WAIST = CIRCLE S: in 4, 3, 2 or 1 line/eyebreak(s). FORMULAS FOR CIRCLE S BELOW:
Circle S4
Circle S3
Circle S2
Circle S1

CIRCLE LONG-WAIST = CIRCLE L: in 4, 3, 2 or 1 line/eyebreak(s). FORMULAS FOR CIRCLE L BELOW:
Circle L4
Circle L3
Circle L2
Circle L1

SQUARE BALANCED WAIST = SQUARE B: in 4, 3, 2 and 1 line/eyebreak(s). FORMULAS FOR SQUARE B BELOW:
Square B4
Square B3
Square B2
Square B1

**SQUARE SHORT WAIST = SQUARE S: in 4, 3, 2 or 1 line/eyebreak(s).
FORMULAS FOR SQUARE S BELOW:**
Square S4
Square S3
Square S2
Square S1

**SQUARE LONG-WAIST = SQUARE L: in 4, 3, 2 or 1 line/eyebreak(s).
FORMULAS FOR SQUARE L BELOW:**
Square L4
Square L3
Square L2
Square L1

**RECTANGLE BALANCED WAIST = RECTANGLE B: in 4, 3, 2, or 1
line/eyebreak(s). FORMULAS FOR RECTANGLE B BELOW:**
Rectangle B4
Rectangle B3
Rectangle B2
Rectangle B1

**RECTANGLE SHORT WAIST = RECTANGLE S: in 4, 3, 2 or 1
line/eyebreak(s). FORMULAS FOR RECTANGLES BELOW:**
Rectangle S4
Rectangle S3
Rectangle S2
Rectangle S1

**RECTANGLE LONG WAIST = RECTANGLE L: in 4, 3, 2 or 1
line/eyebreak(s). FORMULAS FOR RECTANGLE L BELOW:**
Rectangle L4
Rectangle L3
Rectangle L2
Rectangle L1

**TRIANGLE BALANCED WAIST = TRIANGLE B: in 4, 3, 2, or 1
line/eyebreak(s). FORMULAS FOR TRIANGLE B BELOW:**
Triangle B4
Triangle B3

Triangle B2
Triangle B1

TRIANGLE SHORT WAIST = TRIANGLE S: in 4, 3, 2, or 1 line/eyebreak(s). FORMULAS FOR TRIANGLE S BELOW:
Triangle S4
Triangle S3
Triangle S2
Triangle S1

TRIANGLE LONG WAIST = TRIANGLE L: in 4, 3, 2 or 1 line/eyebreak(s). FORMULAS FOR TRIANGLE L BELOW:
Triangle L4
Triangle L3
Triangle L2
Triangle L1

INVERTED TRIANGLE BALANCED WAIST = INVERTED TRIANGLE B: in 4, 3, 2 or 1 line/eyebreak(s). FORMULAS FOR INVERTED TRIANGLE B BELOW:
Inverted Triangle B4
Inverted Triangle B3
Inverted Triangle B2
Inverted Triangle B1

INVERTED TRIANGLE SHORT WAIST = INVERTED TRIANGLE S: in 4, 3, 2 or 1 line/eyebreak(s). FORMULAS FOR INVERTED TRIANGLE S BELOW:
Inverted Triangle S4
Inverted Triangle S3
Inverted Triangle S2
Inverted Triangle S1

INVERTED TRIANGLE LONG WAIST = INVERTED TRIANGLE L: in 4, 3, 2 or 1 line/eyebreak(s). FORMULAS FOR INVERTED TRIANGLE L BELOW:
Inverted Triangle L4
Inverted Triangle L3
Inverted Triangle L2
Inverted Triangle L1

HOURGLASS BALANCED WAIST = HOURGLASS B: in 4, 3, 2 or 1 line/eyebreak(s). FORMULAS FOR HOURGLASS B BELOW:
Hourglass B4
Hourglass B3
Hourglass B2
Hourglass B1

HOURGLASS SHORT WAIST = HOURGLASS S: in 4, 3, 2 or 1 line/eyebreak(s). FORMULAS FOR HOURGLASS S BELOW:
Hourglass S4
Hourglass S3
Hourglass S2
Hourglass S1

HOURGLASS LONG WAIST = HOURGLASS L: in 4, 3, 2 or 1 line/eyebreak(s). FORMULAS FOR HOURGLASS L BELOW:
Hourglass L4
Hourglass L3
Hourglass L2
Hourglass L1

Each volume in *The Book Series* describes in detail three looks per layered Formula, and THREE ADDITIONAL ILLUSTRATIONS by David Russell. So, for instance, 3 examples of Hourglass Long-waisted in 4 layers are detailed in writing, and 3 more are illustrated. 6 *Ideas* for each of the possible layering scenarios of 4, 3, 2, and 1 line(s) are provided for each Body Shape by Waistplacement in their individual book within the series. Also provided, for each Body Shape by Waistplacement, at the end of each book in *The Book Series is* The Shopping list/recap, which includes THE KEY CLASSIFICATIONS of merchandise by Silhouettes that are flattering for the particular Body Shape by Waistplacement, including Coats, dresses, jackets, tops, trousers/Jeans/skirts, swimwear and a brief review of accessories.

THE FASHION INDUSTRIES ANSWER TO DESIGNING CLOTHING FOR WOMEN'S BODIES IS TO AVOID IT, AND TO HIRE THIN, TALL, RECTANGLE OR INVERTED TRIANGLE SHAPED MALE MODELS WITH LONG LEGS AND LONG WAISTS TO MODEL FEMALE CLOTHING.

The Fashion World's answer to sizing is to infer women are just *too* fat. Some Designers assume if all women were skinny, then all problems would mysteriously go away. Magazines are not much better. They stay away from the Waistplacement reality all together. Designers and magazines, at times, address Petites, Plus-sizes and Prices but forget information about the Waistplacement. They also avoid addressing Waistplacements of Short and Long-waisted women. This is the major transformation needed in the Fashion Industry, to really celebrate the beauty of all women.

Another way, in which Designers and manufacturers further avoid the TRUTH about the BODY SHAPE and WAISTPLACEMENT of women, is by hiring male models to wear women's clothing in Fashion Shows. After full investigation, I discovered even the underweight models have Short and Long-waists. (Celebrities and Models are listed in their associating book of The Book Series). Even on Short or Long-waisted models that are modeling standard sizes, in sizes 000, some Silhouettes do NOT FIT their waist length as some are Short and Long-waisted yet tall & skinny.

There is this *given* in fashion that puts all transformation of sizing into the "get skinny" category, avoiding the **UNCHANGEABLE Waistplacement** and its correlating Space of the Waist. These are the challenges women have been living with since the Haute Couture torso dress-form arrived in 1937 and mass production was exploited in 1960. Regardless of minor changes by certain Designers and Manufacturers through the years, only one WAISTPLACEMENT is available in ready to wear today. The clothes are simply cut from patterns by sizes for the Balanced-waistplacement. On the racks today, there is no such thing as a size 6L, Long Waist, or size 8S, Short Waist each Waistplacement in their necessary proportion. This is what is need to intelligently flatter the body.

Size is not inherently comprised of enough information. The Primary Modifier of Waistplacement cannot be ignored any longer. Short-waisted (S) and Long-waisted (L) women need sizes in their proportions too, not just Balanced-waistplacement, sizes, and proportion.

The Fashion Industry's answer to poor fit due to Waistplacement is "Let's use boys to model our clothing for women as they have the Body Shapes we want women to have." The Balance-waistplacement ideal is compromising the entire Industry's ability to service our women of ALL Body Shapes and Waistplacements. The male models and only Balanced-waisted offerings is not an answer for women. Boy models are Rectangle and Inverted Triangle Body Shapes with Long Waists and long legs (oh, yes, and breast free for further convenience). These MALE MODELS for FEMALE CLOTHES offer Designers *their* ideal Body Shape, a shape that is the furthest away from the **Female Body Shape** with its **UNCHANGEABLE Waistplacement**. This is proof of movement away from the AUTHENTIC FEMALE BODY (no offense to the small breasted, long legged, Long-waisted and Balanced-waisted Rectangles and Inverted Triangled women of the world, but I imagine that comprises a group of about 5% of all females in the world). Avoiding women's shapes and Waistplacements is a great defeat on the part of Designers, Labels and Manufacturers of women's clothing across the globe. Women need Short and Long-waisted classifications with their proper proportionate apparel. Eventually, Short and Long Waists will need their own departments. This is the era. This is the time.

This book embraces the TRUTH about THE SPACE OF THE WAIST®. The Waistplacement itself must be included in all categories of sportswear, suits, coats, special occasion, wedding gowns and dresses very soon. It is my intention to inform women, as well as Retailers, Designers, and Manufacturers of women's apparel worldwide, to acknowledge the UNCHANGABLES of the female body. Especially to acknowledge Waistplacement and to provide proportionate apparel by size for ALL women.

Let us state that women, Designers, Labels, and Fashion Leaders need more information. Let us begin with the TRUTH about the UNCHANGEABLES of a woman's Body Shape and Waistplacement, and the Key Factors in Silhouette selection. With this added information in the marketplace this will lead to the transformation of women's sizing.

The sizing would include proper proportions for Short and Long Waists in their offerings along with the Balanced Waists. There is a huge demand for sizing by proportional design or engineering for these 2/3's of women currently being overlooked as they do not fit the Regular Misses or the Petite or Tall profiles.

Retailers can implement these changes **NOW**. Retailers can begin testing Silhouettes for Long-waisted by using their number one selling Silhouettes from their Balanced-waisted assortments. As for example: a fitted dress such as a shirtwaist dress. This can be easily translated for the Long-Waisted designs/patterns and developed in the Long-waisted Silhouette for the Long-waisted woman. Retailers could also develop an item for the Short-waisted women such as a longer and leaner jacket (at least to wrist-length when your arms are hanging down to your sides) without a nipped-in waist. These are just 2 examples of a Long-waisted Silhouette and a Short-waisted Silhouette to develop for market testing.

Fairly quickly Retailers will begin to track their sales and profits in the Long-Waisted dresses and the Short-Waisted Silhouettes. Other departments and classifications of merchandise will follow their lead. Soon other Retailers will evolve their assortments of Silhouettes also. Eventually Retailers will know their sales not only by size and by department, but also by waistplacement. Soon Departments for Short and Long Waists will be part of the Misses mix.

The Wholesale and Retail businesses on all fronts will explode with this extremely necessary transformation. The development of the knowledge into apparel will *either* begin from wholesale offerings introduced by the Designers and Labels to their Buyers or from **Retailers** to their Product Development sources, Designers or Labels. Then when manufactured by the global manufacturing community it will eventually reach mass markets.

This knowledge **and availability** of Silhouettes with B, S and L Waistplacements will create a huge expansion in Retail sales. The idea is Retailers have to begin to become more specific and *less general* in their buying assortments and Designers and Labels must accommodate them. Keeping in mind that most any given Silhouette will not be flattering in ALL sizes (000-18) let alone in ALL Waistplacements (BSL). Instead, prints/patterns and scales should vary with proportions by size. These added selections (soon to become Departments) will increase profits, and finally begin to service the other 2/3's of women.

How wonderful one-day soon, for Long-Waisted women to find classifications of merchandise as for example Dress in their: 0-18 L=LONG-WAISTED sizing/proportion and eventually their own Departments. This is the beginning, as all beginings such as with Petites, Tall's, and Plus-sizes. What a revolution this will be, let us begin... What are you waiting for?

CONCLUSION

Now you know the intention for *The Guide Book* as well as the purpose for *The Book Series* of the 18 Body Shape by Waistplacement books in the series. Below select your book(s) for download/purchase. (You may benefit from two if you are a Borderliner). The different volumes for *The Book Series* are available for those who are interested in improving their knowledge base for dressing a specific Body Shape and Waistplacement. Also, for anyone interested in improving women's fashion and apparel industries, in order to provide the proper apparel in proportion for Balanced (B), Short (S) and Long (L) waist lengths.

LET US REVOLUTIONIZE THE WOMEN'S APPAREL INDUSTRY. THIS WILL RESULT IN RETAIL CLOTHING STORES PROVIDING CLOTHING FOR WOMEN IN ALL WAISTPLACEMENTS, NOT JUST THE ONE REGULAR OR BALANCED WAISTPLACEMENT THAT IS AVAILABLE TODAY.

You know how to discover your Body Shape and your Waistplacement. The measuring techniques have been provided, including my favored one, EMWP.

You may now locate your book for your individual BODY SHAPE by your individual WAISTPLACEMENT from THE SPACE OF THE WAIST® book series. All books within series are listed as follows:

BOOK 1: "The Guide Book" (this book)
YOUR FASHION GUIDE BASED ON BODY SHAPE & THE SPACE OF THE WAIST®

CIRCLES B S L
BOOK 2: CIRCLE BODY SHAPE WITH A BALANCED WAIST = CIRCLE B
BOOK 3: CIRCLE BODY SHAPE WITH A SHORT WAIST = CIRCLE S
BOOK 4: CIRCLE BODY SHAPE WITH A LONG WAIST = CIRCLE L

SQUARE B S L
BOOK 5: SQUARE BODY SHAPE WITH A BALANCED WAIST = SQUARE B
BOOK 6: SQUARE BODY SHAPE WITH A SHORT WAIST = SQUARE S
BOOK 7: SQUARE BODY SHAPE WITH A LONG WAIST = SQUARE L

RECTANGLE B S L
BOOK 8: RECTANGLE BODY SHAPE WITH A BALANCED WAIST = RECTANGLE B
BOOK 9: RECTANGLE BODY SHAPE WITH A SHORT WAIST = RECTANGLE S
BOOK 10: RECTANGLE BODY SHAPE WITH A LONG WAIST = RECTANGLE L

TRIANGLE B S L
BOOK 11: TRIANGLE BODY SHAPE WITH A BALANCED WAIST = TRIANGLE B
BOOK 12: TRIANGLE BODY SHAPE WITH A SHORT WAIST = TRIANGLE S
BOOK 13: TRIANGLE BODY SHAPE WITH A LONG WAIST = TRIANGLE L

INVERTED TRIANGLE B S L
BOOK 14: INVERTED TRIANGLE BODY SHAPE WITH A BALANCED WAIST = INVERTED TRIANGLE B
BOOK 15: INVERTED TRIANGLE BODY SHAPE WITH A SHORT WAIST = INVERTED TRIANGLE S
BOOK 16: INVERTED TRIANGLE BODY SHAPE WITH A LONG WAIST = INVERTED TRIANGLE L

HOURGLASS B S L
BOOK 17: HOURGLASS BODY SHAPE WITH A BALANCED WAIST = HOURGLASS B
BOOK 18: HOURGLASS BODY SHAPE WITH A SHORT WAIST = HOURGLASS S
BOOK 19: HOURGLASS BODY SHAPE WITH A LONG WAIST = HOURGLASS L

INDICES

PROVIDED AS COMPANION INFORMATION FOR THE SHOPPING LIST/RECAP FROM THE INDIVIDUAL BOOKS OF *THE BOOK SERIES* AS A QUICK REFERENCE MOST OFTEN USED IN WOMEN'S CLOTHING AND THEIR VARIOUS SILHOUETTES.

INDEX I - COLOR GROUPS

INDEX II - FABRIC CHOICES

INDEX III - PRINTS AND PATTERNS

INDEX IV - EMBELLISHMENTS

INDEX V - COMPLETE SET OF SILHOUETTES AND DETAILS USED IN THE INDIVIDUAL BOOKS

INDEX I- COLOR GROUPS

CLOTHING SILHOUETTES ARE DESIGNED IN FABRICS OF SPECIFIC COLOR GROUPS (to name a few as there are many various hues) Below are Color Groups that are referenced throughout the 18 books in *The Book Series* of *the Body Shapes by their Waistplacement*. This is a *KEY* reference list for you to refer back to. Many, yet not all, Color Groups and their associating colors are listed below.

COLOR GROUPS:
DARK PIGMENTS: Black, Dark-Inks, Dark Traditional Navy-Blues, Dark Burgundies and Raspberries, Dark Purples, Dark Greens
DARK NEUTRALS: Black, Browns, Grays, Rusts, Dark Navy-Blues, Deep Rich Olive-Greens, Darker Khakis
NEUTRALS: Whites, Off Whites, Creams, Taupes, Beiges, Tans, Khakis, Olives, Mosses and Sages, Pale Grays to Mid-Grays and Browns
EURO-DUSTED DARK TONES: Plums, Blues, Burgundies, Spruce, Forest, Teal and Moss-greens

LIGHT PIGMENTS:
WHITE AND WHISPERS OF COLOR: White; White with Whispers of Lavender, Lilacs, Violets; White with Whispers of Pale Powdery Greens; White with Whispers of Powdery Blues, Aquas or Seafoams; White with Whispers of Yellow to Butterscotch; White with Whispers of Peach
PASTELS: Lavender, Powder-Blue, Mint, Seafoam, Aqua/Blue-Green, Pale Pink, Butter Yellow, Pale Peach
MILKY MID-TONES (mid-tones VERSUS DARK OR PALE milked down with white pigment): Watermelon, Melon, Coral, Pinks, Yellows, Blues, Greens, Blue-Greens
BRIGHTS: Red, Orange, Yellow, Blue, Green, Purple, Pink, Fuschia
NEONS: Fire Red, Flaming Orange, Roaring Yellow, Acid Orange-Yellow, Brilliant Blue, Acid Green, Acid Blue-Green, Acid Yellow-Green, Hot Electric Pink, Ferocious Fuschia, Electric Purple
METALLICS: Gold, Silver, Platinum, Pewter, Nickel, Copper, Bronze, Gunmetal, Rose Gold

INDEX II-FABRICS (some available options)

SILHOUETTES ARE DESIGNED FROM A VARIETY OF FABRICS/FABRIC NAMES (sometimes fabric is used on the reverse).

Specialty Fabrics: High Tech, Water-Resistant, Rubber, Padded, Indigo Dyed, Transparent, Shrunken, Microfiber, Fabrics with Cut-outs or Stenciled Designs, Fortuny Type Pleating, Lacquered Cotton or Lame, Leathers and Suedes, Cellophane and Artificial, Polychrome, Waxed Leather and Waxed Cotton, Plastic, Paper, Bias, Plastic Bodices, Pressed Leather, Chrome-Plated, Vinyl, Quilted, Moiré, Aluminum, Plastic, Ceramic, or Metal Disks knitted into a fabric, Metal and Chain, Batistes, Jacquard Woven and Jacquard Patterns on Patterns or Multi-Colored, Netting, Metallic Threads and Yarns and Metallic "Look a-Likes", Fabrics with Shine, Blends, Synthetic Fabrics, Synthetics and Synthetic Blends, Rayon, Folded and Silver and Metallic Fabric Looks, Cashmere, Merino.

Brocade: Wool, Silk, Rayon, or Cotton

Cottons: (various weaves such as Plain Weave), Twill, Gauze, Velvet, Damask, Dotted Swiss, Gabardine, Satin, Indian, Jersey, Calico Gauzes, Damask, Dotted Swiss, Lacquered, Denim, Gingham, Cotton Satin, Oxford, Pima, Broadcloth, Sheeting, Ottoman, Jacquards, Crochet Pima, Lace, Voile, Tulle

Jersey: Rayon Matte, Silk, Cotton, and poly-blends

Khaki: British Khaki (brought to us by a Kansas City Native Robert Leighton)

Knits: Body Conscious Knits, Stretch Knits

Lace: Tulle, Stretch, Irish Crochet, Italian Needle Point

Leather

Linen

Satin: Satin Crepe

Silks: Georgette, Rayon Jersey, Pongee, Voile, Twill, Georgette, Crepe de Chine, Tussah, Charmeuse, Chiffon, Crepe, Faille, Taffeta, Jersey, Classical Greek Style, Satin, Gauze, Organdy, Jersey (first Madame Gres), Velvet, Wool Blends, Tweeds, Pongee, Gazar, Ottoman, Jacquard, Lace, Tulle, Muslin, Chiffon

Velvets: Rayon Velvet, Velveteen, Silk-velvet

Wools: Alpaca, Serge, Twill, Tweed, Jersey, Gazar, Georgette, Flannel, Double-Faced and Gabardine

FABRIC WOVEN INTO PATTERNS: Wool Tweeds, Donegal Tweeds, Harris Tweeds, Birds-Eye Tweeds, Houndstooth

KNIT WEAVES AND FABRICATION: Rib Knits, Flat Knits, Cashmere, Merino, Cotton, and Alpaca

Many blends: Synthetics, Natural and Synthetic Blends, Rayon, Shiny Fabrics of Natural and Synthetic Blends, Gold, Silver or Other Metallic Yarns Woven into Fabrics.

INDEX III-PRINTS AND PATTERNS

SILHOUETTES ARE OFTEN DESIGNED IN PRINTS OR PATTERNS: PRINTS AND PATTERNS AND ASSOCIATING NATIONALITIES MOST DRAWN UPON FOR INSPIRATION.

PATTERNS AND PRINTS: Animal Prints, Surrealism, Original Cartoons, Celestial, Sky, Earth, Native American, Organic Nature, Scenes, Flowers, Gardens, Insects, Butterflies, Fruits and Vegetables, Everyday Life Objects, Utilitarian, Wave or Oceanic, Reptiles, Trees, Plants, Florals and Floral Motifs in "grand varieties", Pottery Motifs, Geometric Motifs, Psychedelic, Op Art, Modern Art, Poster or Logo Prints, Photography, Plaids, Stripes, Dots, Patchwork, Ethnic Prints and Patterns, Batik Prints, Ikat Prints, Tattoo Prints, Phoenix and Griffin Prints of the Ancient Orient, Deco-Chrysanthemums, Stencil-Printings, Screen Printings, Masks, Arabesque, Bold and Subtle Stripes and Checks, Pinstripes, Abstract Art, Scenes created by Fabrics Sewn Together, Geometric Forms by Fabrics Sewn Together, Handmade Fabric and Fibers, Hand Wovens, Raked or Structural Effects (such as waves, water, crinkles, pleats, pin-tucked made into fabrics), Roped Fabric (or the roping of fabric), Petals, Artistic Textiles and Fiber Art, Hand Painted, Mixed Media, Exotic Pleating, Peacocks, Birds and Feathers, Awning, Animal Skins or Features, Barcodes, Tattersalls, Gingham, Argyles, Celtic Inspirations, Chevrons, Plaids, Trellis and Wreaths.

NATIONALITIES MOST OFTEN USED AS INFLUENCES:
American/Native American, Polish, Austrian, Italian, Romanian, Swiss, Dutch, French, Russian, Egyptian, Grecian, Mexican, Chinese, African, Native American, Asian, Japanese

PERIOD PRINTS AND PATTERNS:
Renaissance, Medieval, Art Deco, Art Nouveau

STRIPES (IN VARYING SCALES AND ENGINEERED WIDTHS):
Candy, Pencils (or thinner), Pinstripes, Regimentals, Romans

INDEX IV EMBELLISHMENTS

EMBELLISHMENTS USED AS DETAILS FOR SILHOUETTES

EMBELLISHMENTS: (Used as details on Silhouettes for interest. Stretch lace and stretch trims.) Plastic, Ceramic or Metal Pieces or Geometric Shapes, D-Rings, Down Feather (quilting and fillers), Feathers, Gross-Grain Ribbons (and other ribbons), Buckles, Taping, Studs, Spikes, Snaps, Laces (Tulle and other), Gold, Silver or Translucent with hints of Color Threads and Cellophane, Peplums, Tulle (and other Sheer Luxury Fabrics), Shirring, Patent, Mirrors, Zippers (plastic/metal colored) metallics, Pom-Pom, Ruffles and Pleats, Crossing Straps, Sequins, Braid, Piping, 3D Flowers, Mesh Backed Beading, Fringes (silk, cotton, rayon, gold silver and other metallics or fabrications), Tassels of various weights and thicknesses, Florals (roses or other floral ornamentations), Netting, Hoods, Fur-Trims (faux or real), Ornamentation (unique to the Designer yet to be named), Pearls (fake or real), Jet (fake or real), Polychrome, Bugle Beads, Diamonds (fake or real), Jewels (fake or real), Cording, Embroidery and Trapunto Stitching, Ticking and Stitching Details, Chinoiserie Floral Embroidery, Lesage embroidery, Pin-Tucks, Boas, Buttons (Wrapped or covered), Appliques, Sashes, Hand Painting, Paneled, Pleated, Greek Inspired "Fortuny" Pleating, Beadwork

BEADS: Metallic beads, Glass, Wooden, Bead Embroidery, Paillettes

INDEX V SILHOUETTES (some available options)

APPAREL IS DIVIDED INTO CLASSIFICATIONS, AND CLASSIFICATIONS ARE DIVIDED INTO SILHOUETTES AND SILHOUETTES ARE NAMED.

FIND A FEW BELOW WITH THEIR CORRELATING OPTIONS AND DETAILS, WHICH WILL BE LISTED AS THEY ARE VIABLE BY INDIVIDUAL BODY SHAPE AND BY WAISTPLACEMENT, IN YOUR INDIVIDUAL BOOKS. Not all Waistplacements by Body Shapes wear the same details and options. Your downloads/purchases by individual book reference only what is flattering for your Body Shape and Waistplacement.

KEY SILHOUETTES IN COATS: Chesterfield, Reefers, Steamer, Trench, Straight Lined, Straighter, Fitted, Semi-Fitted, Longer Leaner, Cocoon, Cape, Cape-let, Kimono, Double-Breasted, Swing, Swing Pleated, Asymmetrical, Hooded, Irregular, Unconstructed (introduced by Giorgio Armani), Military Inspired, Large Back Pleated, Fitted and Flared, Tied or Belted at the Waist, Princess-seamed, Tulip Shaped, Geometrical Shaped (circle, square, rectangle, triangle, inverted triangle)

EVENING COAT: All of the above Silhouettes in dressier, evening fabrics, especially Swing, Straightlined, Hooded, Shawl, and Cape.

KEY SILHOUETTES IN JACKETS: Unconstructed (introduced by Giorgio Armani), Cardigan, Constructed, Blazer, Longer and Leaner, Cocoon, Kimono, "Chanel" (unconstructed cardigan style), Soft-Lined Tailoring, Hard-Lined Tailoring, Menswear Full-Tailoring, Custom Form-Fit, Chinese Shape and Collar, Mandarin Collar, Nehru, Spencer, Smoking, Shawl Collared Wrapped Smoking, Modified Smoking, Eton, Eisenhower, Eaton (straight to the hip), Baseball, Bomber, Bell-Boy, Pea-Coat, Battle (with or without epaulettes), Fly Front Straighter Lined (or various lines), Blouson, Swing, Swing with Pleats, Pleat Front, Pleat Back, Safari, Military Influences, Tyrolean, Norfolk, Empires, Geometrically Shaped (circle, square, rectangle triangle inverted triangle), Fitted, Shaped, Fitted and Flared, Peplum, Shape-Shifters, Semi-Fitted, Fly-Away, Boxy, Trench (with and without the belt or self-tie), Utilitarian and Uniform Inspired, Smocked, Shape-Shifters

KEY SILHOUETTES IN TOPS: Tunic, Caplet, Blouson, Roll-Cuffed, Smocks, Irregular, symmetrical, Western, Bib, Tunic, Cropped, Man-Tailored, Shell, Camisole, Peasant, Halter, Angel, Long and Narrow, Pleated, Crossed, Wrapped, Midriff, *Shape-Shifters*

KEY SILHOUETTES IN SWEATERS: (a major sub-classification of Tops included in Tops in the Book Series). Fanny, Shrink or Shrunken, Tank Top, Tee-Shirt, Tennis Set, Twin set, Wrap, Pullover, Overtop, Flange, Peplum, Blouson, Polo, Henley, Camisole, Cropped, Bustier, Boxy, Letter or other Emblem, *Shape-Shifters*

KEY SILHOUETTES IN DRESSES: Dropped-waisted (**narrow** is the meaning when I use this term; I am not referring to the wide-bodied Dropped-waisted selections. Those are the Partial Dropped-waisted), Fitted, Princess-seamed, Semi-fitted, Body-contouring, Coat and Dress Ensembles (matched sets), Spindle/Body Conscious, Mermaid, Loose-waisted, Wider Dropped-waisted, Chemises, Baby-doll, Poofs, Classic Greek Jersey, Column, Sack, *Shape Shifters*, Empire (under the bustline), Empires (at neckline at shoulder line), T-shaped, Geometrically Shaped (circle, square, rectangle, triangle, inverted triangle/trapeze), A-Lined, Straightlined, Shift, Sheath, Float, Pencil, Shirtwaist, Belted, Fitted and Flared, 2-piece Dress (2-pieces purchased separately but look like a dress when on the body), Architectural-designed, Origami-designs, Draped-designs, Curvilinear-designs, Diagonal and Bias-cuts, Coatdress (cut straight or fitted), Asymmetrical, Irregular and Jumpers.

KEY SILHOUETTES IN TROUSERS/JEANS: All over pleated as "Fortuny" type, Wide Legged, Pajamas, Palazzos, Bias Cuts, Asymmetrical, Paneled, Leggings, Jeggings, Skinny Jeans, Trousers, Jeans, Culottes, Gauchos, Irregular Shapes, Rompers, Jumpsuits, Knickerbockers or (Knickers), Curvilinear Shapes, Harems, Zouve or Dropped Crotches, Straight Cuts, Loose and Banded Bottoms or Slimmer Fit and Banded Bottoms, Toreadors, Cropped Lengths, Capris, Tapers, Walking Shorts, Jamaica Shorts, Short-Shorts, Tapered to the Knees or Below the Knees (evokes a pencil skirt but it is a pair of shorts).

COMMON JEAN SILHOUETTES: (subclass of Jeans/Trousers): Jeggings, Boot-Cuts, Fit and Flared, Very Fitted under the Knee then Flared Dramatically, Straight Legs, Skinny Jeans, Straighter Legs, Bell Bottoms, Highwaisted, Trouser Jeans with Pleats

KEY SILHOUETTES IN SKIRTS: A-line/Triangle/Trapeze (YSL for Dior designed the first dress shape in Trapeze in 1967. It continued throughout all the classifications by Silhouette thereafter), U-Yoked, V-Yoked, Front and Back Yoked, Shirred, Rouched, Gathered, Paneled, Fishtail/Mermaid, Gored, Wrap, Draped, Kilt, Tulip, Crossover, Balloon, Poof, Laser Cut, Madera Worked, Double (or more layers), Dirndl, Trouser-Skirt, Fitted, Semi-Fitted, Pencil, Straight and Straighter Silhouettes, Handkerchief, Ruffled, Tiered, Lettuced, Embroidered, Scalloped, Tuliped Fabric Manipulated Skirt Bodies and Hemlines (and other unlimited embellishments), Bias Cut, Hem Décors (on the body of the skirt or the hem), Zouve and other Dropped Crotch Pant-Skirt, Culotte, Gaucho, Geometrically Shaped (circle, square, rectangle, triangle, inverted triangle), Origami Folded, Linear, Verticals (strips such as "car wash" and other engineered piecing Silhouettes), Rolled, Wired, Twisted, Padded (or otherwise Advanced Illusion custom Silhouettes)

SWIMSUITS: Cut Outs (only limited in design by your or Designers vision), Monokini, Mio, Maillot, Tankini, 2-Piece, Bikini, String Bikini, 1-Piece Topless (Rudy Gernreich 1964), One Piece, Swim Dress, Skirted Bottom 2-Piece (front and back best), Paneled 1 and 2-Pieces (front and back best), Shape-Shifters, Scooped Back (or otherwise detailed backs), Various Bodices and Necklines (to flatter the Body Shape and Waistplacement), *Shape-Shifters*

KEY SWIMSUIT COVER-UPS: Tunics, Smocks, Floats, Irregular Shapes, Asymmetrical Shapes, Peasant Styles, Halters, Long and Narrow Silhouettes, Man Tailored Silhouettes, Kaftans, Maxis, A-lines, Geometric Shaped: (circle, square, rectangle, triangle, inverted triangle)

FLATTERING OPTIONS IN DETAILS FOR COATS, DRESSES, JACKETS AND ALL TOPS

NECKLINES, SHOULDERS AND SLEEVE STYLES AND LENGTHS:

SLEEVE STYLES: Sleeveless, Angel, Roll-Up, Pleated, Long and Narrow, Puffs (at Mid-arm, Short or Capped), Geometric Shaped (circle, square, rectangle, triangle or inverted triangle), Art Deco, Pleated, Cape-Like, Cape, Asymmetrical, Dolman, Roll Cuff, Bell, Bishop, Butterfly, Gigot, Strappy, Straight cut, Medieval-Hanging Style

NECKLINE STYLES: Notched, Wadded, Cowl, Turtle, Mock turtle, Chinese, Mandarin, Wing Collar, Dropped Back Collar (from kabuki costume influence), Long Narrow, Jabot, Rolled Collar, Bowtie, Stand Collar, Halter, Veed-Neckline, U-Necklined, Square, Boat/Bateau, Hoods. Shoulder Empire (gathered at the shoulder from which the body of dress flows), Neck Empire (gathered near the neckline or halter neckline from which the body of the dress flows), Empire (under the bustline).

SHOULDER STYLES: Arched, Square, Rounded, Oblong, Pointed, Raglan, Dropped, Padded, T-Shape, Curvilinear, Cape, Cape-Like, Asymmetrical, Off-Shoulder, Set-in-Shoulder.

SLEEVE LENGTHS: Bracelet, Cap, Long, Mid, Elbow, Short, Sleeveless

VARYING CUFF TYPES: (Coats, Dresses, Jackets and Tops) Slanted, Roll Sleeve, Double-Cuff (or more cuffs)

NOTES:

NOTES:

NOTES:

NOTES:

AUTHOR BIO

C. Melody Edmondson is an author currently residing in Tucson, Arizona. Melody had a fast-paced career in the Fashion & Retail Industry in Buying, Merchandising, Product Development, and Fashion Direction.

Her insight into the way clothes fit the female body, and the fact that clothing manufactured today is in only one WAISTPLACEMENT has passionately led her to promote THE SPACE OF THE WAIST®.

She hopes to encourage the Fashion and Apparel Industry to provide women of the world all Waistplacements, including Short and Long-waisted all in their correct proportions. Her work led to the discovery that it is the Waistplacement, not weight, that is the *KEY* to dressing well and loving the body you have!

OTHER BOOKS BY THE AUTHOR WITHIN THIS SERIES

Available on: www.amazon.com/author/melodyedmondson

Book 1 – The Guide Book:
Your Fashion Guide Based on Body Shape and THE SPACE OF THE WAIST®

Book 2 – Circle Body Shape with a Balanced Waistplacement

Book 3 – Circle Body Shape with a Short Waistplacement

Book 4 – Circle Body Shape with a Long Waistplacement

Book 5 – Square Body Shape with a Balanced Waistplacement

Book 6 – Square Body Shape with a Short Waistplacement

Book 7 – Square Body Shape with a Long Waistplacement

Book 8 – Rectangle Body Shape with a Balanced Waistplacement

Book 9 – Rectangle Body Shape with a Short Waistplacement

Book 10 – Rectangle Body Shape with a Long Waistplacement

Book 11 – Triangle Body Shape with a Balanced Waistplacement

Book 12 – Triangle Body Shape with a Short Waistplacement

Book 13 – Triangle Body Shape with a Long Waistplacement

Book 14 – Inverted Triangle Body Shape with a Balanced Waistplacement

Book 15 – Inverted Triangle Shape with a Short Waistplacement

Book 16 – Inverted Triangle Body Shape with a Long Waistplacement

Book 17 – Hourglass Body Shape with a Balanced Waistplacement

Book 18 – Hourglass Body Shape with a Short Waistplacement

Book 19 – Hourglass Body Shape with a Long Waistplacement

Made in the USA
Charleston, SC
27 December 2015